Blue Tiger

Ascending the Min is slow, dangerous, and difficult.

Blue Tiger

Harry R. Caldwell

COACHWHIP PUBLICATIONS
Landisville, Pennsylvania

Blue Tiger, by Harry R. Caldwell
Coachwhip Publications. 2007. All rights reserved.
Published in New York, 1924. No copyright renewal.

(ISBN) 1-930585-38-1
(ISBN-13) 978-1-930585-38-6

SK233 .C3
799.5 C14

Coachwhipbooks.com

Contents

LOVINGLY DEDICATED TO
BELLE COPE CALDWELL
MY WIFE
AND TO
MY CHILDREN
WHO HAVE BEEN MY COMPANIONS
IN THE STUDY OF GOD'S GREAT
OUT-OF-DOORS

Introduction

Late in the afternoon of a steaming summer's day in 1916 my wife and I were being rowed up the beautiful Min River in Fukien Province, south China. On the opposite shore a squalid village climbed from the water's edge into the smothering vegetation of the mountain side. As our half-naked boatmen swung the heavy junk across the river, gradually the massed humanity on the bank took shape. Blue-gowned men, tiny naked children, and women with silver knives flashing in their hair materialized from the drab background of mud and stone. Among them strode a tall man in a white pith helmet, moving restlessly up and down the steps and along the water's edge. We could see that he was built like a well-trained athlete; that he was nearly six feet tall and that a flashing smile seldom left his face in repose—intensely alive, bursting with enthusiasm, strenuously active! That was the quick impression of Harry R. Caldwell which registered on my mental retina even before I stepped out of the boat and grasped his hand.

I had come half around the world to join him in the tiger country of southern China, and what manner of man he was meant much to me. In an instant I knew that all was well, that this rifle-bearing missionary was a real "he-man." At that moment, seven years ago, there began a friendship based on those enduring qualities of mutual interests, respect, and admiration.

I have hunted with Harry Caldwell, have lived with him in his family, have seen him in his mission work, and know his life. In many respects he is one of the most unusual men I ever have met. His skill with a rifle and as a field observer is hardly less remarkable than his ability as a missionary. Through it all runs the vital energy and intense enthusiasm that I felt when I met him first on that river bank in southern China. He never does things by halves. Indeed, it would be impossible for him to do a thing at all unless he threw himself into it physically and mentally with all his force.

It is hardly necessary to say that his missionary work, the great object of his life, has been a marked success. I will not speak of it from the evangelical standpoint, but rather from the broader effect he has had upon the community and the province. Thousands of Chinese who have not come under the influence of his spiritual teaching know him by reputation. Courage, honesty, broad-mindedness, and fair-dealing appeal to the Chinese as they appeal to people of every country of the earth.

Harry Caldwell stands for those qualities. He represents the type of man who is needed in the mission field as in every other walk of life. To the people he comes to teach he brings deeds as well as words; something to grip their imaginations; something physical that they can admire.

I always picture him with a rifle in one hand and a Bible in the other—using the rifle not only to keep himself fit physically and mentally, but also as the wedge to force open the walls of superstition and idolatry, that he may drive home the Great Truth to which he has dedicated the fullness of his youth and life.

Roy Chapman Andrews,
   American Museum of Natural History,
   New York City, N. Y.
   April 2, 1924.

I

A Rifle as a Calling Card

The Chinese are probably the most punctilious people on earth. Let no man think that he can win their confidence or friendship without careful attention to the niceties of social custom.

It has been my privilege to serve as a missionary in China for twenty-four years. During that period I have been stationed in five different cities and have been responsible for the extension of the Christian enterprise into many previously untouched portions of the province of Fukien. It has been my effort, of course, always to conduct myself and my work in such a manner as would meet with the approval of the Chinese in those regions. But I have found, to my astonishment, that what I undertook as a means of relaxation has again and again proved my most direct passport to the confidence of these people.

It is a strange thing, this matter of being known as a hunter. I little suspected, as a boy in the mountains of Tennessee, where the squirrel-rifle is much more of a daily comrade than the slate or the arithmetic, that the time would come when that same rifle would prove a means for advancing the knowledge of the Christian God in the heart of Asia.

Still less did I dream that the interest in flowers and all manner of living things, born in those boyhood days amidst the rioting beauty of the Southern highland, would prove for me an opening sesame to the fellowship of great scientific societies and of some of the world's noted naturalists.

Yet that is just what has happened. There are at many points in China to-day flourishing Christian congregations that trace directly back to the time when I went into those neighborhoods with my Savage rifle. And much interest has been aroused in a part of China that is off the beaten routes of travel by the collections that I have made in the course of thousands of miles tramped over those hills and that now are exhibited in half a dozen museums of America.

Often, as I think back, it seems the merest chance that my work as a missionary should have developed along these unusual lines. It was a bishop who started me on what many of my friends would have called a useless side line. I had come to the East, like so many other young recruits, full of energy and with more devotion than judgment. I was strong, as any graduate of the Tennessee mountains was likely to be. I was determined, in the words of the Methodist ordination service, to "apply all diligence to frame and fashion my life according to the doctrine of Christ and to make an wholesome example." That meant that I was tempted for a time to refrain from such frivolities as tennis, tea parties, and other amusements in which I saw some missionaries indulging. Such a course meant that I should give all my waking hours to an intense preaching of the gospel. By so doing I felt that I was setting an example of what a good missionary should be. As a result, one day during my first year of full-time service I woke up to find myself in bed.

I was sick, mentally and physically, in a lonely place. And right here let me say that I believe that there has been much useless squandering of priceless human material by some missions through sending workers into spots where they had no contacts other than with the people with whom they were supposed to work. When young missionaries are sent from the myriad contacts of life at home to the isolation of some mission station that is supposed to contain but a single family, the mental strain becomes so great that again and again the worker either breaks under it or withdraws. This is what had happened in my case. Many mission boards now sense the inefficiency of this policy and are concentrating their workers in larger groups, but there are still cases in which men and women are sent where they must bear alone the many burdens of the mission station.

Just so I often lay in bed at my semi-isolated mission station feverishly wondering whether the end of my dream of service on the foreign field had come and, at times, even fearing that I might have reached the end of my service in any land. And then to me there came the bishop.[1] It was the session of the Annual Conference which brought Bishop Bashford to my station and very vitally into my life. After he had talked with me long enough to discover what had really brought my troubles upon me, out of the richness of his experience he counseled me to climb back on my old Tennessee hobbies and ride them once more in China. I date any real efficiency on my part as a missionary from that day.

I have never gone out of my way to hunt tiger or other big game except when on vacations. I have never allowed my interest in flora or fauna to interfere in the slightest with my interest in the establishment of the kingdom of God in this part of the world. But these other interests came along naturally, and, as I say, have not only proved

-----

[1] Bishop Bashford, to whom this reference is made, was a bishop of the Methodist Episcopal Church, stationed in China from 1904 to 1918.

my own physical salvation but have contributed largely to the major end I have had in view, which has always been to exalt Christ and his love.

Let me illustrate how the thing works. For years I had longed to preach the gospel in a certain strategic community. I saw that I had to crack the shell of that particular community or abandon the evangelization of an area of more than one hundred towns and villages with half a million souls. Attempt after attempt to enter this region was blocked just when it seemed that success was at hand. There was bitter prejudice against the foreigner and all his works, consequently, the doors of the community had been sealed so long that the exclusion of foreigners had become a matter of pride among the elder clansmen. This condition might have remained unchanged until this day had not a man-eating tiger appeared upon the scene.

In their desperation, after many had been killed, the elders of the clans appealed to me through a dignified delegation to come and dispose of the tiger. A few months before I had shot an especially troublesome tiger in that vicinity. Of course I responded eagerly. I took with me both my Bible and my rifle, for I was bent upon a twofold mission in this long coveted field.

Courtesy would have it that I be entertained in the home of the elder who had extended the invitation to me. This was the opportunity for which I had long waited. My host was the elder of the clan which felt that it had suffered unjustly at the hands of a missionary of a foreign church and it was in this home years before that the feast was given sealing the covenant to block any foreign religion from gaining a foothold. If I could break down prejudice in this home, I knew that the other doors in the region would be opened wide.

As soon as I had settled in the elder's home I pulled out my tiger gun and began to try its action. The gun itself interested the people much, but the little sharp pointed cartridges even more. I was using a twenty-two caliber, high-power Savage rifle at the time, and the people could not conceive that such a light weight gun and such a small ball would be effective with an animal such as I was after. Excitement ran very high.

That evening conversation centered largely around a little cartridge which would bore a hole through half an inch of iron. Every male member of the family was jammed into the room, while the eyes or ears of its female members were pressed close to cracks or knot holes. I kept the conversation going at top speed, waiting for some person to express an opinion of the gun in such a way that I could use it to lead to other matters.

The following morning the opportunity came. A score or more of men from neighboring homes had come in to see the gun. Here in this home, as in almost every home, there were farm implements, looms, and many other things. Seeing a plow in a corner, I declared that the little gun would shoot straight through the iron at a distance of one hundred yards. Accepting a challenge to make good what I had been saying, half the village followed me to the hill back of the house. In the crowd were not only young men and children reckless in their excitement but the long-gowned *literati*, who followed with the slow, sedate swing characteristic of their class. When I fired, my claim was more than proven good.

Upon returning to the house many remarks were made about the rifle, but as yet nothing that would serve my purpose. Six more cartridges were jammed into the magazine and rapidly thrown out. A young scholar turned to the elders who were seated around tables, sipping tea, and exclaimed: "This is truly a strange gun: as compared with our own guns, it is very much better."

That was the comparison idea for which I had been waiting. Following that lead, I talked for a time concerning guns, pointing out how my gun excelled.

It is often difficult to suppress wholly the feeling and attitude of superiority when discussing things that have come from our own country and of which we are justly proud. But this is necessary when talking to a crowd of scholars in China, unless one wishes to alienate his hearers. With as much humility as I could summon, I began to enlarge on the excellent qualities of my gun and then told how there were excellent qualities in other things manufactured in America. As it was harvest time, I could talk about the American reaper which does the work of several score Chinese harvest hands. It was not difficult to get my listeners to agree that such a machine was better than the sickle.

My crowd was still holding together, though restless at times. When I saw the restlessness beginning, I would play the action of my gun, throwing cartridges in and out of the magazine until they were all again close around me. Finally, at what seemed the psychological moment, I boldly said: "Friends, you agree with me that this gun is better than yours and that the American farm implement is better than those with which you cultivate your fields and harvest your grain, and when you have listened to what I have to say about the 'Christ doctrine' you will see that it too is better than the religions of your fathers."

To my delight, not a foot shuffled on the floor. The next hour was given up to a friendly discussion as to the merits of Christianity. I showed that the worship of the Christian God was based upon love, while the worship of most of the popular idols my hearers knew was based upon fear. In defense of this statement I appealed to first one and then another, asking if it was not fear which prompted him to prostrate himself before the idols in the community temple or to burn incense and joss money before the home altar. My arguments were effective. Every man agreed with me, and, what is more, before leaving this village there was extended a pressing invitation to open both a preaching place and a Christian day school. Christianity had won a definite footing in a hitherto hostile community. It had been an effective preaching of the gospel of Christ with a rifle as the text.

In the same way many a fervent gospel message has been hatched out of some chrysalis or cocoon. If there is animate life in these things, so there is spiritual life in a message preached from just such a simple text. It is no difficult thing to borrow from Mother Nature a text which will get you across to a people as inquisitive as the Chinese, who are always ready to see what the foreigner has in his hand or hear what he has to say.

In April, 1910, I was passing through a community where the day before a tiger had killed a sixteen-year-old boy. I will not take the space here to tell the story of the way in which I killed the animal in its lair at very close range. It is of interest, however, to see how the killing of that beast turned almost an entire village to Christ.

The dead tiger was carried in by eight men and placed in the open court of the house belonging to the leading elder of the clans comprising the group of thriving villages. After stationing guards to protect the animal from being picked to pieces by the people, who attach great importance even to the whiskers or hairs of the tail, I retreated to the guest-room of the house and began to clean my gun. Soon the room was jammed with people eager to hear the story of the shot and to see the weapon.

The people in this community knew little about the purpose of the missionaries in China. They were bitterly prejudiced, however, on account of some wild rumors that had been spread to the effect that foreign doctors steal the eyes of Chinese dead for use in concocting some kind of medicine. I am sure that, had it not been for my position as the avenger of the death of the sixteen-year-old boy, there would have been no avenue of approach for me into the confidence of these people. I began to talk in defense of Christianity and the presence of missionaries in China, openly attacking the old system of placating the gods. I soon had the more irreligious and indifferent laughing and jeering at those who stubbornly clung to ancient ways. In this my method was one of bold attack. My frankness and the appeal to their own reason and judgment soon gained for me an inspiring hearing.

It was not until five minutes before midnight that I put my gun into its case, thus announcing that I was through talking. A few final questions were asked as we hurriedly packed up my things preparatory to starting off, with eight strong men bearing torches and the tiger.

A few weeks later a delegation from this community waited upon me, requesting in the name of the elders of the clans that a preacher be assigned to tell them more of a God who loves people. The best that I could do for them was to open a Christian day school, and to delegate an earnest local preacher as its teacher. During the day children were taught and at night adults.

I was standing on my lawn in the upper end of the province late one evening five years later talking with the celebrated naturalist, Roy Chapman Andrews. We were watching the play of the sunset on the broad expanse of the river below us. Our conversation concerned the wonderful fauna of Fukien. Andrews and I seldom talk long about anything but the fauna of somewhere. A lot of bats scurried across the skyline, whereupon we began to talk about bats in general and this species in particular.

Our plans had been completed for starting in a few days for the Futsing region to spend a month in research work and especially to hunt for the so-called "Blue Tiger." Our talk about bats recalled to my mind a temple in the village where we would establish our first camp, where I had seen several genera of bats.

"I can catch you a bushel of bats," I said to Andrews, "in less time than it takes to tell you about it in a temple close to where we will first pitch camp." Then I proceeded to tell him of the sport I had repeatedly enjoyed, drumming upon the pillars of the temple and watching the bats fly out in masses that almost darkened the door. There was, accordingly, included in our outfit for the expedition a lot of bat-catching paraphernalia.

On July 4th we pitched camp in an orchard close by the village where I had killed the man-eater five years before, and within one mile of the lair where on two occasions I had seen a beautiful "Blue Tiger" at very close range. On the following morning I suggested to Andrews that we make a reconnoiter for signs of tiger. But Andrews said: "What about the bats? Let's get the bats first."

Accordingly, we opened one of the iron-bound trunks and took out nets which were to be spread across the doors of the temple. As we walked through the grove of gum trees I declared with confidence that it would require but a few minutes to secure all the bats that the taxidermists could handle.

The temple stood in a deep grove at the head of a flight of steps that had formerly always been like polished stone on account of the constant wear. Now there were weeds growing between the stones.

Upon reaching the terrace upon which the temple stood I saw only a pile of ruins and much debris. Several large idols still sat upon pedestals where once there had been an altar. The temple had disappeared. My chagrin was complete, as I confessed to Andrews that we would have to look elsewhere for our bats.

After disposing of our paraphernalia again in camp, I slipped away to the home of Elder Ding to inquire of him what had become of the village temple. At my question he looked at me in blank astonishment for a time and then merely said, "Teacher, you surely must understand."

"Understand what?" I demanded.

"Why, teacher, can you not understand?"

I assured him that I did not understand at all what he was talking about and again asked him what had happened to the once artistic temple.

"Why, we decided that we did not need the temple after we learned the 'Christian doctrine,'" said the Elder. He then went on to enlarge upon how the people had broken away from idolatry family by family, and, pointing to the beautiful little brick church a mile away, he said: "Our people would rather seek soul happiness over there than in the temple."

Before we ended our conversation Elder Ding remarked, "Teacher, I am afraid those people would not have heard of Christ until this day had you not killed that tiger." Again a gun had been used to preach the first sermon in a community of villages.

II

The Hill of the Mystery Cats

A hill, or, in fact, two hills with a quiet little valley between, marks the end of a rugged range of mountains jutting out of the coastwise range of Fukien where it is broken by a broad and fertile plain through which runs the south branch of the Min River. Over the divide, or saddle, between these two hills winds a footpath which for centuries has been the connecting link between teeming life far back in the fastness of the rugged mountains and the so-called civilization of the plain and the world beyond—that bustling world of which Foochow City is the center. This path cuts diagonally across the valley between the hills before being lost among the villages skirting the plain.

For centuries the traveler along this path has seen many kinds of what are called wild cats and denizens of the wilds in the valley and upon the sides of the hills. As the shadows lengthened at the close of the day the abandoned terraces and well-kept grave sites have been the playground for the young of the "mystery cat." These animals have enjoyed an immunity much more effectual than any that could be provided by a code of game laws written in statute books, and consequently have increased greatly in number and kind.

It was not always so, however, for these so-called "cats" include the civets, wild dogs, and foxes, all of which have

worked great havoc among the small pigs and poultry of
the peasant people. Porcupine, pangolin, and small deer
are also here in abundance, all with marked medicinal
values, so it is safe to say that at one time hunters frequented this region with bow and gun. But things suddenly changed one day; the gods changed them, and streaks
of bad luck among the more daring hunters finally established the fact that these animals were not flesh and blood
at all, but evil spirits incarnate in the denizens of these
wilds!

After many unsuccessful attempts to kill these animals
a group of pious hunters appealed to their god, *Hieng
Tieng Siong-da*, to share with him the kill of the hunt of
the First Moon. The favor of the god having been solicited
by elaborate sacrifices upon his altar, accompanied by
the burning of quantities of incense and joss money, the
spokesman for the group of waiting hunters bowed himself to the earth, three times striking his head with a thud
upon a slab of stone at the feet of the god. This he did to
signify the importance of the occasion. He then grasped
the divining blocks, tossing them high in the air. They fell
just right the first throw. The god was pleased with the
offering made, and was now ready to pronounce blessing
upon the hunt.

After further routine and necessary ceremonies, a container made of a large bamboo joint in which were just
one hundred slender splints of bamboo consecutively
numbered, was picked off the altar. By that peculiar
motion acquired only by practice from childhood, the one
hundred slender splints in the container became possessed of life, each climbing forward as if taken with a
desire to escape as the intercessor poured out his petition
before the god. No sooner had the petition ended than one
splint toppled out and fell upon the floor in front of the idol.

Without paying any attention to this splint the peti-
tioner again picked up the divining blocks, and with the

question, "Is this the proper splint?" tossed them high in the air with a twirling motion which caused them to rest at far different points. The blocks now rested at opposite corners of the altar, one with the flat and the other with the oval face up. Again favorable answer had come with the first throw. Surely the god must be kind to-day.

The whole thing amounted to this—that the bamboo splint still on the floor in front of the god bore the right number, that is to say, the number that conveyed the will of the god in this particular matter. Now all that remained was to consult the "Prayer-answer Board" and ascertain what the god had to say about this particular hunt.

In the larger and more frequented temples this board is not used, but in its stead is a waiting priest to stand before the wall of numbered "pijin holes," each containing the answer to a prayer. In this instance there was no priest to stand as middle-man between the hunters and their god, so the spokesman eagerly picked up the splint to ascertain its number, inviting all who could read to assist him in deciphering the answer.

Crestfallen, the hunter turned to his friends and announced the hunt abandoned. The answer of the board was unmistakable.

The number happened to call for a quotation from the classics against the taking of life, a mere snatch from the writings of some ardent Buddhist. What else could it possibly mean but that the god had claimed protection for these cats? These hunters suddenly realized how near they had been to sacrilege. These were not cats at all, but spirits, "fox devils" which cannot be killed, and whom to harm is hazardous.

Since that day in the long ago the superstition about spirit cats has grown as mold grows, until the very life of the ignorant people of this part of China has become blighted. The woman into whom has entered one of these spirit cats is as popular as the priest and must be consulted on every imaginable occasion. She is a diviner of spirits and interpreter of omens and dreams. Unto her is committed the fate of the living, and in her is the voice of the dead. As Saul consulted the witch in the days of his trouble, so do the benighted people of China commit their all into the hands of her into whom has entered the spirit of a devil cat. This female conjurer and spirit medium decides the destinies of millions of people, while foxes and wild cats enjoy an immunity due to a superstition stronger than law.

It was during the month of March, when dykes were being repaired and fields flooded preparatory to the spring planting of seedling rice, that I crossed a broad expanse of plain and approached a desolate-looking village tucked away between two groves of camphor trees. This was one bit of country into which I had never penetrated, though by the natives I was credited with having traveled every wild animal trail of all that vast hill country. My visit at this time was to accompany a noted naturalist and get him adjusted for a few days of field work.

As we crossed the plain we heard from a community of villages hard up against the foot hills the incessant blowing of conch shells, beating of gongs, and the shouting of children and men. I immediately interpreted this bedlam as meaning that a tiger had recently made an attack upon an animal or man, which proved to be the case.

The famous "Blue Tiger," which no white man except myself has ever seen, during the previous few months had claimed a heavy toll of lives in this immediate neighborhood. Fifty deaths were also charged against him in a nest of villages just across a low divide. I hoped we had connected up with him again.

There was great excitement when two foreigners armed with "tiger guns" entered the community unannounced. Everyone began to talk tiger, and to tell of a cow which had just been killed in a dooryard. Our party consisted of Mr. A. de C. Sowerby, the noted naturalist, who has done so much really worthwhile scientific research work in China, now representing the National Museum at Washington, his cook, and a taxidermist; Da Da, my faithful Chinese traveling companion for more than eighteen years, and tried scout on many an adventure, and myself.

I cared for but little other than getting the scientist comfortably established for his work. My plans were to start back on the following day. Burden-bearers were already engaged to meet me at daylight, when I would take up the march. More than once I have felt decidedly unhappy in China in not being able to devote time to research work with specialists who have come to me with some special field in view. On this occasion it was imperative that I hurry right on to meet some important engagements more than one hundred and fifty miles away. In matter of time that means much in China.

On the evening of my stay in this community many hunters and woodsmen gathered in the dingy little room we were occupying to look us over, but more especially to see our guns. The conversation naturally drifted along the line of hunting in general, but tiger hunting in particular.

Incidentally, I mentioned the fact that there were signs of but few so-called wild cats in the neighborhood. One of the hunters suggested the presence of so many tigers might explain the absence of the smaller carnivores, a conclusion at which I had already arrived. Tigers abound in the foot hills bordering the cultivated plains where cat life is plentiful. The cats enter the fields by well-defined runways and it is an easy matter for tigers to ambush them along these burrows.

The ten or more Chinese hunters were soon debating their experiences among the "spirit cats" of some near-by hills. This subject was suggested by one of their number bringing in a fine mink, which was very much prized by Mr. Sowerby. I listened with interest to this conversation concerning black cats, spotted cats, ring-tailed cats, striped cats, and, in fact, many animals that were not cats at all, all of which it was impossible to kill.

Being well acquainted with the superstition concerning "devil cats," I inquired the whereabouts of these so-called "spirit" or "mystery cats." In response to my inquiry ten or more hunters broke into animated conversation, each trying to tell the most thrilling story of how he had shot daylight through one of these animals without so much as making an impression on it. They all described how, at the base of a certain big bowlder, these cats suddenly disappeared upon being fired at, or when too hard pressed by the dogs. Such a common occurrence was this, all declared, as to give the place the name of the "Disappearing Rock." There were hunters to vouch for every yarn spun, but the one about the "disappearing" of the cats received universal corroboration.

"I have stood on the top of that big rock and had big cats run almost under my feet, only to see them suddenly disappear as I leveled my gun," one burly woodsman exclaimed.

A big fellow to my right shouted in response to this, "Yes, I was standing beside you one time when this very thing happened, and another time I saw you shoot a big hole right through a 'spirit cat,' after which it only ran away the faster."

So the discussion ran along until well into the evening. I tried to explain away the thing on the grounds of its being a mere superstition, but to no avail. It was too evident that these men believed implicitly in what they were saying, and it would have been unwise for me to carry my arguments too far.

My friend Sowerby had already tucked himself comfortably away in his blankets, and I was anxious to crawl into my sleeping bag too, for the night was raw and cold. To get rid of the crowd I finally hooted at the whole "mystery cat" proposition and turned to unlacing my hunting boots.

One daring hunter advanced, and looking me straight in the eye said, "Teacher, dare you go with us among these cats? Come and we will make you eat your words."

This invitation suggested to me a wonderful opportunity, so I arose, faced the spokesman, and accepted the challenge. I stipulated certain conditions, however, but to all these every hunter readily agreed by a shout of approval or by the bowing of the head. As I felt that here would be an opportunity to shatter the most binding superstition known to the hunter folk in southern China and one that might never confront me or any man again, I agreed to remain over another day and join in a hunt for the "mystery cats."

The whole conversation was carried on in the Foochow language, wholly unknown to Mr. Sowerby, who was born in a missionary home in the north. When the hunters had pretty well scattered, Mr. Sowerby spoke from among his blankets, "Caldwell, what under heavens is all this about?" I explained the situation, and the conditions upon which I had agreed to remain over another day.

The agreement with these men on their part was that they were to connect us up with the cats and give us such fair shots as they claimed they always had. If we killed the animals, they were to abandon forever their belief in the so-called "fox devil," and were never again to consult the temples and shrines in order to ascertain the will of the gods regarding the hunt. It was agreed on our part that if either Mr. Sowerby, Da Da, or I got fair chances and did not kill, it would prove the animals were not flesh and blood, and I would "eat my words" spoken against the theory of the spirit cats.

After the crowd had dispersed and as we were quietly settling down for the night in the darkness of a windowless room, Mr. Sowerby broke the silence, saying, "Caldwell, when you think about it there is a serious aspect to this thing, for if we should shoot and miss you have identified yourself with the believers in the 'mystery cats.'"

I had realized all that was involved, and just what it would mean if we shot at the animals in question and missed, but I went peacefully to sleep that night, realizing that there was that upon which I relied for success the following day other than either skill or luck. I had absolutely no concern over the outcome, provided the cats were actually up and on the move, as we had been assured. To me this appealed as one of the greatest opportunities for some practical preaching of the gospel I had ever met in China.

It was a motley lot of hunters and dogs which struck the trail on that March morning in 1922 toward the hills in the distant haze, the recognized home of the "devil cats." There were sixteen hunters following us as we left camp a little after dawn, and behind the hunters a long line of curs sufficient in number to rout out anything along the line of march.

When three miles along the trail the leading dog dashed off into the tangle of some abandoned terraces and routed out a small animal. Both Sowerby and I fired at the scurrying spotted figure in the tall grass and missed. No matter how we may have felt about the miss, the hunters attached no importance to it whatever, for this was not on the "forbidden" hills. The animal was passed up as one of the civets or mongooses, and nothing more was said. A mile or so further on we approached the twin hills which were pointed out to us as our goal.

Upon reaching the saddle between these hills the hunters, splitting up into two groups, held a hurried council. Fifteen men started off for their positions in the drive, while the other man led us a little to the right and assigned us our stands on the most frequented runways. I purposely chose the big stone at the foot of which the animals always mysteriously "disappeared," while both Sowerby and Da Da took stands at likely points.

Hardly had the signal for the drive been given when the dogs opened up on the opposite slope. Sure enough, the cats were on the move. In fact, they were very much on the move. From my vantage point I saw one large spotted animal hurrying along a trail leading our way, while another large red animal broke into the open, where it paused long enough to locate, the dogs and then skurried back into cover. Things soon became intensely interesting and we were all on the alert. I had never known anything like it before for wild animals. The tossing of a stone into almost any bramble seemed to put something into motion. From my position I could enjoy it all.

The first thing to come my way was announced by a chorus of shouts from ten or more hunters lined up on the opposite slope. As the animal hurried along the run leading toward the "disappearing rock" the excitement among the hunters broke all bounds. I was intent upon neither permitting the animal to slip by me nor to "disappear" at the foot of the rock.

I could now plainly see by the position of the pointing fingers and guns that the animal had approached to the very base of the rock, still I had not heard so much as the rustle of a grass. Naturally, for I could hear nothing on account of the din kept up by the hunters across the way. Much was at stake and the tension was really high. The animal had had worlds of time to break cover either above or below the rock, but still I had not heard a sound.

Suddenly the hunters ceased shouting and there was dead silence. The thing they had predicted would happen had happened—the animal had "disappeared." One man broke the stillness by shouting, "The cat has become not already; why fool any longer?"

At this instant I heard the rustling of grass far to my left and below. Turning I saw a streak of red flash across an opening between two small pine trees. A snapshot at long range caught the animal in midair. With the first shot, I had killed one of the "mystery" animals protected so long by the gods.

The little beast had done exactly what might have been expected. It had doubled back over the ledge to fool the dogs and had broken away at right angles down the hill. Right here was where the "disappearing" had taken place all these years, but now the spell was broken.

As the hunters gathered around the animal I had killed, and carefully examined it to make sure it was flesh and bone, Da Da's gun banged away on the top of the hill. Then followed even greater excitement among the hunters up there, for he had killed one of the "spotted cats" through which daylight had so often been shot without so much as altering its pace.

I climbed back upon the top of the big stone which had played so important a part in the superstitions of the community, around which had gathered a large group of villagers and hunters to examine the animals killed, and talked to these people for half an hour concerning their blind beliefs in devil-spirits and goblins. The kill was enough to more than seal the covenant with the hunters, but the villagers were still bold in their assertions of the way in which these cats "fly over the roofs of buildings and catch pigs and fowls."

After reaching camp I had another hour of talk with the hunters concerning the futility of many of their superstitious beliefs, and then turned in, feeling the result of the day's hunt could not be measured by the several very fine scientific specimens we had taken. In the morning I again addressed a large crowd of men, women, and children seated around the coping of the "Heaven's well" of the home where we were staying, and found the people eager to listen to any message. No one offered a word in defense of the long-cherished beliefs about the "disappearing" or "devil cats." Once again a gun had served the purpose of gaining confidence and getting in a message much more effectively than any amount of abstruse preaching could have.

III

Solving Some Chinese Puzzles

During my first year in China, when I was trying to acquire a working knowledge of the language, I spent much time with my teacher studying bird life in the olive orchards and small groves marking grave sites around Foochow. This was an intensely interesting field for study, as there were so many surprises in the comparative study of the birds of China with those of eastern North America. Time and again I would find what seemed to be an interesting parallelism, only to have my findings overturned by carrying the study a little further.

When I found the lesser tit (*Parus minor*) I was for a time fooled into thinking I had run across the friendly little chickadee of Tennessee. I searched every possible nesting site in hollow trees adjacent to my home for several seasons trying to carry the study to its limits by a careful comparison of nesting habits and eggs. It was when I found this dainty little bird nesting in a hole in a mud bank, or crevice in the foundation of a stone wall but a few inches above ground, that I realized my bird education had been seriously lacking somewhere along the line.

Hirundo, the swallow, which, in the homeland, seeks either the high timbers of an isolated barn or a secluded spot on an overhanging cliff for a nesting site, is happiest in China when its mud home is plastered just over the low door on a busy street front, or saddled to a peg inside the

30

house hardly out of reach of the babbling inmates. I have never known a swallow to build its nest in an unoccupied house in China, while no house can be too noisy to serve as a home site.

There is a certain superstition among the Chinese people concerning the return of the swallow to the ancestral home from year to year, and it is exceedingly difficult to secure even one set of swallow eggs for scientific study. For years I tried to buy sets of swallows' eggs in Fukien province, but without avail. Being exceedingly anxious to secure at least one set for a museum in California I finally resorted to preaching a sermon on superstition in a community largely Christian.

My theme gave me ample room for a real gospel sermon, for the Chinese are pretty nearly as superstitious as are the people of America. They do not attach any special importance to Friday, it is true; nor do they worry much when thirteen people happen to be seated at a meal, nor is the first snake of spring crossing their paths of special significance, so far as I have been able to ascertain. Instead of the good-luck horseshoe over the door of a Chinese home we find a sprig of thorny cactus to keep the devils out, or a bit of idol paper for good joss. But the emotion is just the same whether in America or China. The only noticeable difference is in the way it manifests itself.

So, when I needed the swallows' eggs I preached with all my power against superstition, supporting my argument by relating the experience I had for twenty years trying to secure sets of swallows' eggs. I declared that even Christian people seemed to fear they would offend some skulking spirit or goblin, or would break a good luck spell by disturbing a swallow's nest.

The result was amusing. Within an hour there were brought to me many sets of fresh eggs, half sets and singles. There were eggs just ready to hatch, and I pleaded, without avail, to have these returned to the nests.

These people—men, old women, and children—understood nothing about the blowing and preserving of eggs, so it was useless to talk to them about advanced incubation. Their only thought was that the eggs were for the compounding of some kind of foreign medicine, and the state of incubation made but little difference. Protest was no use. I had to accept the eggs or offer offense, and on that day I completed with a vengeance my study of the swallow, and got eggs to answer all possible purposes for all time to come.

Early in my career in China I became much interested in the saying among the Chinese, "When the wild dove lays three eggs, the third one hatches out a hawk." My scholarly teacher was well acquainted with the saying, as was my coolie boy, and both had the same explanation, so I knew there must be some foundation to the saying which had become a proverb. My object was to find out what there was to give rise to such a belief, and as I carried the study further and further the thing became a riddle to me which seemed beyond solution.

For years I fairly haunted the nesting sites of the common Chinese turtledove, finding the birds nesting in brambles, in trees, and in holes in the retaining walls of graves, but I could never find the nest containing three eggs. In my eagerness to solve the riddle I went after the other and far more rare species of wild dove, running down every species of dove nesting in the province, yet I found no trace of a nest containing either three eggs or three young.

I had now, it seemed to me, run down every possible clue and was just as far from a solution of the problem as the day I began. The thing began to get on my nerves, for ask whom I would, all would declare the truth of the statement about the third egg of the dove. While I was thus balked in my efforts to find any solution that would serve as ground for the saying, still I was just as much resolved to find the dove that would deign to mother a hawk as I had ever been during a period of more than ten years' search.

The thing dragged on for a number of years until one glorious summer morning I was standing in the open between a little grove and two wide-spreading banyan trees. I had located a dove's nest on a low branch of the banyan the previous day, but this interested me little, as I had been locating nests of the kind for the past ten years, none of which ever contained more than two eggs.

I was studying at this time the courting habits of the beautiful dayal bird (*Copsychus salauris*). This bird fairly goes mad with song when trying to win from a rival singer a modest colored mate. One bird had taken his stand upon the point of a dragon's tail decoration on the roof of a near-by temple and was pouring out a volume of sweet song, when a common cuckoo darted from the grove and glided toward the banyan trees. The two singing suitors were too busy to notice this, but, in response to the sharp alarm call of the lesser tit, the bird upon the dragon tail dropped like a stone to earth and hid in the foundation of the temple. A general alarm now went up from all the birds in the thicket, and I thought how utterly foolish the little things were in thinking the cuckoo a merlin, or small hawk.

As silence now ruled where song had been riot a few seconds before it occurred to me that somewhere in this little drama was the solution of the riddle which had so long bothered me. A later visit to the dove's nest proved that I was correct. There were the two partly incubated eggs of the dove and the newly laid egg of the cuckoo. The riddle was solved.

The Chinese people are slow in making observations but all too quick in arriving at conclusions. A real naturalist would be difficult to find, except among those who have been well trained through association with foreigners in field work. Yet there is not a phenomenon in nature study which has not an accepted explanation. Almost any child will tell you all about the wasp or bee which does not have young of its own but steals the young of others and rears them. There is always some fact to give foundation to such accepted sayings. I had heard this thing talked about by scholars and even preached about from the pulpit, but it was not until after years of observation in China that I saw the so-called "kidnaper," or "Ang Pung," in the act of "adopting" for itself children.

One afternoon I was crouched among the gnarled roots of a spreading gum tree with rifle in hand waiting for the movement of a tiger in its lair. There was a constant humming of mud wasps about my hiding place. So intent was I in watching for the tiger that I paid but little attention to the wasps as they brought in their little mud bricks and whined their weird song as they carried on their work like true masons.

This went on for more than an hour without making any impression upon me, but as a gorgeously colored wasp came across my front dragging a paralyzed cicada I forgot for the moment the tiger and began to think of pirate, and then of kidnaping. It was all very plain now. I had located the much-talked-of "kidnaper," as later investigation proved. The Chinese philosophers in ages past had watched the so-called "potter wasp" at work bringing a store of crickets, spiders, larvae, and so forth, in a stupefied condition for food supply for its young, and had jumped at the conclusion that these things were to be reared as adopted children. Another riddle had been solved.

One of the noisiest yet most interesting places one can find in China is the early morning market. In the larger cities the market is conducted in a low shed covering several acres of ground space and is a daily occurrence, while in the interior of the province stalls are built either on a covered bridge conveniently near densely populated communities or counters are improvised in front of houses and shops in the larger villages. No village can claim a right to market day out of turn, and but little business is done except on that day.

In Foochow there are many markets, but possibly no street is busier than the one paralleling the river on the Nantai Island side. Early one morning I was standing on a hill overlooking the Min River near the American Consulate, studying all the habits of the lesser tit, the nest of which I had at that time not succeeded in locating. At the foot of this hill, which breaks off almost precipitously, is a very busy section of the market street.

As I stood upon the cliff enjoying the chaffering over all kinds of wares there was a rustle of wings overhead. Looking up I saw the nest of a black-eared kite in the top of a tall, overhanging pine tree. The great variation in color of the eggs of this hawk has offered me a very interesting study, so I decided to climb the tree and examine the contents of this nest.

The climb was long and tiring. When about half way up the tree, and while clinging in a position where it was impossible to defend myself, the old kite viciously attacked from above. At the first swoop she struck my head with great force, fastening her strong talons in my cap, making away with what she supposed was my scalp.

The bird made straight away across the river, tearing at my cap with her strong beak. When nearly across the river she wheeled and, upon seeing me still in the tree, uttered a loud shriek and dived straight at me again. I had now reached a limb and was able to offer defense, and so did not worry much.

Below me in an open space was the usual rabble and bustle attending the early morning market. A group of people were in what seemed to be an especially spirited wrangle over a basket of vegetables fresh from the gardens. As the hawk got right over the street she released my cap and made a swoop at me. The cap glided down through space, landing squarely upon the basket of vegetables. I was so interested in seeing what was going to become of my cap I almost forgot to defend myself, sustaining slight scalp wounds.

There was sudden silence among the wranglers below me. First, every eye was turned toward the cap, and then twenty or more brown faces were looking into the open heavens above. Seeing nothing but the blue vault, the crowd dispersed as if a lighted bomb had landed in their midst. The basket of vegetables was abandoned, protected only by the cap which had come down from the gods. Though always ready to explain every phenomenon, no Chinaman that day was able to explain to the satisfaction of his brethren how a foreign devil's head gear dropped into a busy market place from the heavens above.

The legend concerning the so-called "pass-over-hunger-grass" in the stomach of a tiger evidently has come down from early times as a result of a blade of grass found in some tiger killed. It is commonly known that not only dogs but cats eat grass blades for medicinal purposes. I was very much discredited at one time for trying to convince the public that two animals were tigers, neither of which, when opened, possessed the wonderfully efficacious blade of grass. The gentry standing around when the animals were being skinned were bidding high for the blades of grass, but upon finding there were none announced with disgust that the animals were not true tigers. As usual, the ignorant rabble believed them.

The sages offered this blade of grass as an explanation why tigers often leave parts of their kill uneaten. They claimed that because of the benevolent spirit of the tiger, which prompts it to leave the head and parts of a kill for some less fortunate of its kind which on account of old age or otherwise is unable to kill enough to maintain it, the gods have placed in the stomach of this king cat this blade of grass, which oozes out nutrition so that the kindly animal is thus protected from ever suffering from hunger.

It was not until I had killed these two fine specimens and skinned them in the presence of several noted scholars that I learned the origin of the grass supposed to be in a tiger's stomach. But I also learned that day that, rather than proving the emptiness of such a belief, the absence of grass in the stomach only went to prove that the animal parading under the guise of a tiger was an impostor.

The Chinese character meaning "lord" or "emperor" must also be found in the markings of the face of a tiger if it is to be a real tiger of whom devils and demons are afraid. I had shot one handsome male tiger with two horizontal and one vertical white lines in the forehead not exactly to the liking of the scholars, and this animal too was discredited. Such a one is said never to have been born of tiger parents, but to have emerged through some strange metamorphosis from some animal or fish living in the sea.

It is these little things with their attending relations to the lives of the people among whom one lives that break the monotony of life for one living almost beyond the bounds of civilization. Both folklore and nature study are full of much that will enrich and enliven life through observation and study, and sometimes it is the little things which are of greatest interest. The solving of so-called Chinese puzzles has proven a pleasant pastime to me. I recommend it as an antidote for grouchiness.

Plate 1

1. There were plenty of mothers who were ready to bear testimony that this brute was a child eater, even though the scholars did discredit his being a real tiger on account of the markings of his face. The animal had killed and eaten a man only a few hours before it was killed in its lair.
2. This "hog-nosed" badger is one of the animals enjoying immunity for years on account of the superstition about the "Mystery Cats." It is a rare specimen, very important from a scientific standpoint. It is closely allied to *Arctonyx leucoloemus*, of the northern part of China.
3. Armed with primitive fowling pieces these hunters stand as soldiers on guard around a son of the hill genii which a "foreign devil" has been bold enough to kill. Though afraid to molest the animal when alive, they barter and even fight over flesh, bones, and blood of the victim.
4. Pangolin carrying its young.

Plate 2

1. The soldiers and attendants of the "Emperor of Hell" blocking the procession in order to prevent me from photographing them in action. The order was given by the director, who may be seen in the middle of the group to "bunch" around the "Emperor" in order to save him from the indignity of being photographed. (Later a liberal "tip" got the whole crowd to pose for a picture.) The soldiers charged me, when to have fled might have proven a very serious matter.
2. It is indeed an important occasion that will tempt the great "Emperor of Hell" to participate in person. In the picture this chief of evil spirits is seen riding upon a horse with one side of his face white, signifying he rules in the realm of the living; the other side black, showing he rules in the realms of the dead.
3. The band too, has halted to shout back a warning to some god about to enter the city gate. It is more than child's play when one goes out intent upon getting the pictures of gods.
4. Each constable bears some sign of the death he died, signifying his rank in the distinguished order of "Vengeance Wreakers." One has a plate driven deep into the skull, showing that he died by violence at some feast; another a knife cleaving the head, etc. So real is this counterfeit as to completely fool the common people into thinking these are indeed those whom they must appease in order to escape the ills of life.

Plate 3

1. The part of "Tall Brother" and the "Monkey Devil" for the most part seems to be to go through stunts and antics which are of a reassuring nature to the people who have been subjected through fear by the more serious aspects of the procession.
2. This woman has for forty-one years lived true to the man whom she married the day after he died, and upon the day she was to have been married to him.
3. Gods are created for the occasion and at the order of the spirit medium. There was raging a terrible siege of cholera in Foochow when the mediums ordered the elders of the clans to place guards at the launch landing to keep the "cholera devil" from landing off the daily launch running between Foochow and this place. Images were hurriedly built of rice straw and planted in the field near the launch landing. To them was assigned the task of expelling the devils if they landed. Behind them waved a large flag which served as insignia of authority.
4. The "devil" did land and slip through this cordon of guardian gods and wreaked terrible vengeance upon the community bold enough to offer such an affront to the constable from hell having this cholera matter in hand.

Plate 4

1. It is necessary to constantly repair the tow-line, a mile or more of which is in the hold of every large boat.
2. Always on their guard with strong bamboo poles, two expert boatmen man the front of the boat. By hurriedly wrapping a length of rope attached to the gunwhale around the pole and thrusting the lower end against a hidden rock, it is possible to fairly lift the boat out of danger, this being done by a deep counter sweep of the tail oar.
3. The pull of the current against the line as the trackers take their position is great. While position is thus being taken three men on the front deck of the boat are hurriedly examining and repairing the line.
4. One of the most difficult problems is that of preventing the boat being swung against the rocks, where the current sweeps around a point. Here again the two men at the front play their part while others heave and push to the accompaniment of a great deal of grunting and calling upon the river goddess for help.

IV

The Tiger at Home

Civilization, primitive and crude as it has been, attended by the destruction of the growing timber, has forced all China's big game inland to retreats more secluded than the almost barren coastwise mountain ranges now afford. It is a common thing to hear the elders of the clans talk of the days when both the serow and wapiti, or some other form of very large deer, were common on hills now almost denuded of growing timber, while both leopard and tiger abounded to a far greater extent but a decade or so ago.

It is not home-building, nor the agricultural pursuits of this present generation that have so devastated the mountain fastness, for everything seems to indicate that this wonderful hill country was once more thoroughly cultivated than now, while the deserted hamlets and brush-ridden ruins indicate that there has been a decided scattering of a once dense population among the foothills. Two factors, at least, have contributed largely to existing conditions in South China.

In the first place, there has been within the last few decades an exodus from this mountain and hill country on account of the movement toward the larger centers and cities. Many able-bodied men now seem to find greater satisfaction serving as chair bearers or ricksha coolies in the cities than they did tilling the soil on the ancestral homestead. With this movement toward the larger centers there has been an attending moral degeneration, for the young men from the rural sections have found it hard to withstand the temptations always met among city environments, thousands returning to their ancestral homes physical and moral wrecks.

During this same period, and more especially during the past ten years or so, there has been an ever-increasing stream of emigrants seeking homes and employment in the Malay States and beyond. This movement has been encouraged by American and British missionaries living in those parts, who have sometimes even acted as agents in organizing colonies of Fukienese to work on the rubber plantations and in the tin mines. Even a greater degree of degeneracy has resulted from this mass movement of Chinese to distant points, this being especially true of those who work in the mines. On the other hand, the Fukien Chinese Christians who have followed these movements have proven themselves to be of such character as to become practically the hope of a strong and enduring Malaysian Church, under the wise guidance of the missionaries stationed in these great centers.

Whilst the congested conditions have seemingly been greatly relieved by this exodus to other parts, those who have remained by the homestead of their fathers have been subjected to extreme hardships little dreamed of in the earlier days. The natural results of the deforestation ruthlessly carried on in generations past are now being realized, to the sorrow of those living in the ancestral homes, for, with the possible exception of very limited areas, the people are reduced to terrible straits by the frightful shortage of fuel. The burning of wood has long since become out of the question with the masses living along the coast, as the hills are absolutely barren of trees. Here and there hills covered with seedling pines are permitted to attain a height of ten feet or so, but then they yield to the terrible fuel pressure and are harvested and marketed at some distant center at astonishingly high prices.

The natural outcome of this policy is that the masses living along the foothills and in the adjacent plains are being compelled to rely for their fuel supply upon the grass growing upon the hills, which is especially rank in the ravines. Along the coast even grass roots are pulled up during the stage of low tides and among the salt marshes. These are washed several times to remove the mud and salt and burned sparingly in the preparation of food.

Among these people there is no provision for even such comfort as the fire-basket affords. This is used commonly where there is a growth of trees sufficient to permit the burning of charcoal. The actual suffering due to this fuel shortage is intense, as the price of wood and coal brought in by the sea is prohibitive. Peat beds here and there have been found from which "coal balls" are made, offering some relief to those who have access to such fuel and can afford to burn it.

Just when the hardwood and pine disappeared from these barren hills would be difficult to ascertain, but the many hills, standing out in bold relief, without so much as an inch of soil, would indicate that it has been many years since the disastrous work of deforestation became complete. The mountain ranges further inland seem doomed to the same deplorable fate. It has been told me by raftsmen that more than ten million dollars' worth of logs are rafted down the Min River annually. No country can long stand such a draining off of its timber life.

One would hardly expect to find tigers among the almost barren hills along the coast of Fukien Province, but it seems that the king cat of these wilds reluctantly abandons this region where it has fared well for ages, though now only here and there may be found ravines sufficiently wooded to offer shelter from sun and storm. It is from such centers that the marauders issue forth to carry on their work of destruction among the flocks and herds of the peasant people living among the foothills and on the plains. It is also during these twilight excursions that the greatest loss of human life occurs.

On many occasions I have spent one or more days in the region infested by both leopard and tiger, and interesting indeed have been many of the stories I have heard. Availing myself of every opportunity to make a first-hand study of the habits of tigers in this comparatively open country, during a period of more than ten years I have time and again been richly rewarded for the time and risk involved.

I have been especially interested in the doings of a tiger long talked of by the natives as the "Black Devil," but which I later termed the "Blue Tiger." On two different occasions and at very close range I have seen specimens of this peculiarly marked and handsome animal. While seeking opportunity for a shot at this particular tiger I have repeatedly concealed myself behind a "blind" in the lair and made long studies of the habits of tigers of the regular type when they had no reason to suspect the presence of an enemy.

In March, 1910, I led a goat into a ravine where had frequently been seen tigers of the ordinary type. A number of wood-cutters had reported having seen the blue tiger in this lair, so it was with hopes of seeing a specimen of this type that I entered the ravine. I was armed with a double-barrel shotgun, instead of my usual Savage rifle, as it was by chance only that I was passing through this tiger-infested region.

On this occasion the tiger responded immediately to the bleating of the goat tethered on an abandoned terrace. For more than an hour the tiger was in full view, not to exceed fifty yards away.

It seemed to suspect treachery on account of the lone goat being in this out-of-the-way place. Had it been the

fleet little muntjac, with which the mountains abound,
barking for its mate, the tiger doubtless would have made
an immediate attack lest the animal slip away. As it was,
the big cat sat for nearly an hour like a huge tabby, repeatedly putting forward the front foot as if to move forward,
but each time drawing it back to its original position. I
have never been able to make other studies which reflect
any degree of certain light upon why this tiger acted in
such a cautious manner. Others watched have advanced to
their kill rapidly under much more unfavorable conditions.

While watching this tiger I learned one very important
thing concerning the nature of an attack. I noticed that
the cat followed the trail instead of taking a much shorter
cut through the tangle which would have landed it directly in attacking position. Subsequent observations have
proven that a tiger always follows a path, or takes the
course of least resistance, even though by so doing it is
necessary to make a wide detour. It will not work its way
over rough and uneven ground or through unbroken
tangle.

The study of this animal was completed after it crossed
a depression and came out upon some barren ground
across which it was necessary to work its way before the
final attack. It was now within a few rods of the goat, and
seemed to realize that it was very much exposed. But to
secure the goat it had to cross the open, and cross it he
did, more like a great striped serpent than a majestic beast
of prey.

With head extended so that chin and throat touched
the ground, and every muscle seemingly strained, the
animal propelled itself along with amazing speed with
absolutely no motion other than what appeared a mere
quivering of the shoulders and hips.

This study did not last long, however, for just as soon
as the tiger was under cover of the terrace he made three
flying leaps, each landing upon the point of a terrace,

and bringing him to the foot of the terrace upon which both goat and hunter stood. As the animal crawled upon the upper terrace and settled catlike for a final spring it saw me at a distance of not more than twenty-five feet. Without paying any more attention to the goat the animal squared itself toward me. At this point it became necessary for me to fire the shot that finished this wonderful study.

A tiger by instinct is a coward. Bold and daring, when circumstances favor him, he will hurriedly abandon a fresh kill of a goat or a cow upon the first cry of a shepherd boy attending a flock perhaps a long distance away. There is no animal which hunts its prey near the habitation of man which seems to weigh conditions before making an attack as does the tiger. If things do not exactly suit his liking, no amount of coaxing with a live bait will, tempt him to venture into the open.

One handsome tigress lay for three hours in plain view on a grassy terrace a few hundred yards from the bleating goat without offering to attack. When she finally made up her mind, she moved rapidly forward along a trail until within striking distance, when she was dropped with a single shot.

An experience I had in April, 1910, illustrates this point. I had led a goat into a ravine where a tiger was known to be which had been working havoc among the herds of the farmers. A day or two previous to my hunt it had attacked a herd of cows, killing three, but abandoning them upon hearing voices several hundreds of yards away.

Upon the occasion of my hunt the great cat suspected mischief and moved with caution. Advancing along a covered trail to within thirty yards of the goat, he halted to make a survey before the final dash. Peering into a valley he saw two men cutting grass more than five hundred yards away. Apparently fearful lest he expose himself, the huge beast, after taking in the situation for a time, turned and vanished noiselessly in the bush. I made this study from a blind of grass not more than fifty feet from the tiger. It is when close enough to study the very expression on the face, so to speak, that one feels repaid for risk and effort.

A few days later this same tiger awaited an opportunity to attack the cow with which a farmer was plowing his field. The farmer had unhitched his cow from the yoke and was squatted upon a dyke not ten yards away eating a midday lunch when the tiger charged from the near-by brush, killing the cow where it stood behind the man. All of which went to show how daring the animal may sometimes be when it can strike from behind.

On several occasions I have known a tiger to attack a goat or cow being led by a tether-rope, killing it instantly, while the man leading the animal was frantically tugging at the other end of the rope. Both tiger and leopard frequently rush a dog or pig standing inside the open door of a house amid all the confusion common to a Chinese home. In practically every instance of this kind which has come under my observation, the animal has been killed, though the tiger has not always succeeded in carrying it away.

Daring strategy and slinking cowardice characterize the tiger as perhaps no other animal of the wilds. Often after securing his victim, courage seems to fail and he abandons the kill, bounding off into the nearest bush.

Two men hunting deer not far from my home disturbed a large tiger from its bed. The animal made a dash at the man standing nearest in line with its path of retreat, seized him by the lower leg, and dragged him into the ravine below. Luckily, the man succeeded in grasping a small tree, whereupon the tiger released his hold, leaving the man almost paralyzed with pain and fear.

At a point near Futsing city a group of men gathering fuel on the hills routed out a tiger on a grass-covered terrace. The enraged animal turned upon the group, crushing the skull and neck of two and striking the third a blow which landed him lifeless on the terrace below. The animal did not attempt to drag any of the dead men into the cover.

Near Yenping City a father and his small son were walking along a trail in 1920 when a notoriously fierce man-eater attacked the lad, fixing his strong fangs in the skull, and made off into the brush. The hysterical father followed the tiger, shouting and calling for help. After making good an escape, the tiger released the boy, not offering to attack the father. The animal followed a path around a hill where a man was working in his field two hundred yards away. He killed this man but made no attempt either to devour him or to drag him away.

The strength and vitality of a full grown man-eater is amazing. I had an occasion to spend a night in a village where a tiger had performed some wonderful feats. Just at dusk he entered the village and located a cow and yearling calf in a pen adjoining a house against the hill. This pen had been made by excavating the hill, and could be entered only through a door from the back of the house. The tiger lunged from above into the pen and killed the heifer, attracting the attention of the inmates of the home, who raised a great commotion and threw open the door into the cow pen just in time to see the tiger and his kill disappear with one graceful leap to the top of the embankment. There was no way for the tiger to get the heifer out of the pen except by throwing it out bodily or by leaping out with it in its mouth, either of which courses required a great deal of strength. I measured this embankment and found it to be twelve feet high.

The same tiger attacked a hog dressing two hundred pounds and made away with it a distance of more than half a mile before being overtaken. When the hog was found it had no wounds or bruises except the deep fang wound in the neck. Evidently, courage had again failed after the brute had made well away with his kill. The villagers declare that when a tiger is making off with a heavy load he seldom attempts to drag his prey, but throws across the back bodily and rushes off with grace and ease.

One of the finest trophies I ever took around Foochow was killed in May, 1910. This beast had but a few hours before killed and eaten a sixteen-year-old boy. I happened to be passing through the country, and decided to attempt to dispose of the troublesome creature. Securing a goat with two small kids I worked my way well into the lair to a point near where the boy had been eaten. The goat was tied in the open at a safe distance from any path, while the kids were put in a large basket and buried in the grass well up in the lair near where the two trails crossed.

The very fact that when hunting tigers in this way one at all times feels he perhaps is himself being stalked adds a great deal to the hunt and keeps one upon his mettle. To relax even a little in one's vigil might prove disastrous. I was very much upon my guard during this particular hunt, taking every precaution to forestall any surprise attack. Being well acquainted with the paths and trails of the lair, I was comparatively safe unless I made some foolish blunder. My thought was that the tiger would approach stealthily along some one of the trails so long as he could not see his prey, and it was for this reason I buried the basket containing the kids in the grass, for it would be necessary for me to shoot the tiger at very close range, and it was to my advantage to have his attention riveted in the direction of the bleating kids. It was upon these calculations alone that I could hope for a successful shot.

Approach as he might, the animal would have to be within twenty yards of me before I could see him. For more than two hours I sat perfectly still, waiting, alert to every movement or sound, and concealed only by a frail blind of grass and ferns. There was nothing to break the awful silence other than the incessant bleating of the goats supplemented by the unpleasant rasping call of the bamboo partridge from the bush. The tension was so great at times that the crawling of black ants in the dry leaves sounded like the moving of some large animal in the brush.

Hope had about given way to despair when suddenly there emerged from the overhanging grass the huge head of the man-eater exactly where I had figured he would appear, and not to exceed fifteen yards from me. Within fifteen feet of the kids he was stealthily moving forward, with head, neck and back in about the same plane. I had seen a number of tigers in the wild, but never an animal even approaching this big cat, just a few yards away, intent, alert, but heedless to all else save the locating of the bleating kids. I have often wondered what would have happened if this animal had suddenly spied me crouching in the grass so near him.

I would have given a great deal to have been in a position to permit this study to go on a little further, but it seemed important that I kill the animal before he killed me. Though I had implicit confidence in the gun I was using, I realized how dangerous a proposition it is to come to quarters in such a tangle with such an animal as was before me.

Raising my rifle I took hurried aim and fired. The sportsman can find no other occasion to pull the trigger where there is such an attending thrill as when tiger hunting under such conditions. At the crack of the gun the huge beast settled forward with hardly a struggle, within a few feet of the kids he had located and upon which he was about to spring. The animal proved to be a handsome male weighing a little more than four hundred pounds.

Upon hearing the shot and being assured that the tiger was dead the villagers swarmed into the ravine, each eager not only to see their tormentor dead, but to gather up the blood. In fact, but little attention was paid to the tiger until every available drop of blood had been sopped up with rags torn from the clothing, while men and children almost fought for the blood-stained grass. The blood of a tiger is very highly prized for two purposes. A bit of blood-stained rag is worn about the neck of a child as prevention against attack by measles or smallpox devils. And, too, it is claimed that a bloodstained handkerchief or rag waved in front of an attacking dog will flag the animal, causing it to turn tail and retreat.

I recall what happened only a short distance from where I was behind a blind waiting for a tiger. Instead of attacking the goat, which had doubtless attracted the tiger to the spot by its incessant bleating, the beast attacked a cow feeding in the open. Two little shepherd boys who were sitting upon the top of a big rock playing "Jack-stones" raised a murderous yell which aroused a cur asleep at the base of the rock. The dog rushed off in the direction of the cow, which was down and struggling with a broken neck, and, before realizing what the real trouble was, came fairly upon the tiger, which had retreated a few yards and was standing under a little cover. Upon seeing the tiger, the dog turned to run, bounding wildly part way across an open space to fall prostrate from fright, dying where it fell.

Chinese hunters have been much interested in what I have told them about the proposed expedition after the so-called "Blue Tiger" with a pack of American bear hounds, declaring that the tiger would only revel in slaughter if surrounded by attacking dogs. It must be remembered that the favorite food of tiger is dog flesh, and it would first become necessary to educate the animal a little concerning both the vicious attack and method of defense of the trained American hunting dog. My opinion is that any pack of dogs would suffer terribly while this schooling was going on. If I had a pack of ever so well trained dogs I would much prefer letting them give vent to their pent-up energies by chasing mountain lions than by loosing the leash after a tiger amid such surroundings as the tangled and grass covered terraces of Fukien Mountains.

That Chinese dogs are cowed at the very scent of a tiger is evident. When taking a fine tiger specimen to Foochow on a steam launch I saw a well-dressed *literati* come forward and sop up the blood oozing out upon the deck with a silk handkerchief. Seeing that I was much interested in what he was doing, the scholar said to me, in a rather apologetic manner, "Teacher, I can turn the attack of the fiercest dog by waving this bloody handkerchief in front of him."

From the Chinese point of view the skin is not the most valuable part of a tiger. Almost always before a tiger hunt or drive is made, or before a pen or pit is prepared for trapping an animal, the hunters burn incense and offer sacrifices before the gods in a temple, or at some shrine, and solemn covenant is entered into to the effect that if the hunt is successful the skin of the trophy becomes the property of the god. Thus it happens that in many temples may be found handsome tiger-skin robes spread in the chair occupied by some god having to do with the chase. Both the god known as "Duai Uong," or god of the land or place, and the "Pearly Emperor" have thus become the possessors of far too many handsome tiger and leopard skins.

The flesh of the big cat is very valuable for medicinal purposes. When a hunt is successful it often happens that several cows are killed and the flesh mixed with that of the tiger, all then being sold at the exorbitant price which is cheerfully paid for tiger meat.

The bones of a tiger are boiled for a number of days until a gelatine-like mass is produced. This is sold at very high prices as an exceptionally efficacious medicine. I have often been urged by interested professional friends to take a little of this product to strengthen me for my long tramps over the mountains, being assured that a piece as large as a bean mixed in a cup of tea would serve as guaranteed insurance against becoming fatigued even during the most trying tramps.

The results of the few days I have been permitted to spend at intervals and under varied conditions studying the tiger in his habitat have produced in me a profound respect for the brute, even though he be a thieving man-eater. His Majesty of the Wilds is quite a different proposition from the cowed and inert tiger of the zoo.

V

A Summer's Experience with Tigers

It is customary for the families of both missionaries and foreign business men in north Fukien to spend a few weeks during the intensely hot season of each year at some point in the mountains where the children can escape the prickly heat, and to which the fathers may retreat for the weekend. Conditions arising during the spring of 1911 rendered it necessary that I should devote considerable attention to certain special interest in connection with my work during the summer season, for which reason I found it difficult to get away with my family to the accustomed resort near Foochow. Accordingly, I planned to take the family into the hills somewhere on my own field, finally selecting a large and almost deserted monastery among the mountains to the west of Futsing City.

It was by the merest accident that I learned of this interesting place, secluded in one of nature's most picturesque retreats. Up to the time of my first visit no white person had ever been seen there. I was therefore a bit timid about seeking quarters for my wife and family for a period of a month or more during the summer, but the welcome extended me by the priests soon dispelled all misgivings, and assured me that we would not be regarded as intruders.

As a rule, the priests like to have foreigners visit the monasteries on account of the tips and tokens they leave in the hands of the man who acts as guide, or interpreter of the history and wonders of the place. But in this particular instance it was the reputation I had won as a tiger hunter that prompted both priests and hangers-on to extend the second hand of welcome, for the place was overrun with tigers. Several of these had turned man-eater and were a menace to everyone living in the great bowl which included within its boundaries two small villages and many scattered homes, in addition to several temples employing the services of fifty or more priests.

The fact that I was erecting a fine stone church in a large market town not many miles away first suggested to me the possibility of seeking summer quarters in this secluded place. But when I visited the place and heard the people whispering among themselves that possibly I would be brave enough to undertake to dispose of some of the troublesome tigers I definitely decided to remain.

Late in the winter of the year I broke away from the plain, with its half a million people, and started toward the monastery, where I hoped to secure summer quarters. I headed into the mountains, following a well-paved road under an avenue of wonderful liquid amber trees, and along a plunging stream for a distance of three miles. This trail was the approach to the innermost recesses of as beautiful hill country as one ever sees.

People whom I passed halted and looked long, invariably breaking out with some remarks about tigers, when they saw that I carried a gun. The sun had not yet set, so I hastened my steps, thinking possibly that I might be able to get in a tiger hunt at dusk, provided all this talk about tigers along the approach to the monastery was even half true.

I found all kind of evidence that there were tigers in the great bowl, and, though I had walked twenty-five miles already, I hurriedly got things adjusted for the night while my cook bargained with the head priest for the spending of the summer at the place. All this done, we secured a goat to serve as a bait and hurried off toward what seemed to me to be the most likely lair for tigers. Throwing myself upon the ground beside a trail to take a breathing spell while my cook tethered out the goat, I looked across a wide depression and beheld the most wonderful specimen of tiger I had ever seen, standing upon the top of a bowlder, looking steadily at me. The distance was not too great for a shot from my high-power rifle, although the light was anything but good. Taking careful aim, I tumbled the animal off the bowlder with a single shot. He proved to bear all the ear-marks of a real old man-eater.

After returning to the monastery I began to congratulate myself upon so soon disposing of this huge beast, since I had definitely decided to spend the summer there, only to be assured by all present that there were "Plenty tiger in lair, all same man-eater like this one." Plans for taking my wife and children to such a place began to be attended with considerable misgivings. But I determined to go through with the adventure.

Upon arriving at the monastery with my family in the summer we found many things to enliven our spirits. We had opportunity to study Buddhism to our hearts' content. The local form of this religion revealed more and more absurdities each day as we had opportunity to become acquainted with the practices of the priesthood. The contrasts with Christianity became more marked as we studied the many methods adopted in order to pacify devils and demons.

All this was most interesting, but I confess I lived every day under a vision of horrors, for I did not know what instant a tiger would pick up one of the children. I could not go on with my other work until I had made a thorough study of each lair in order to ascertain whether or not there were tigers then occupying the big bowl. Investigations were not carried very far before both my cook and I found many convincing signs. It now became necessary in some way to dispose of the animals before life could be considered safe even right around the monastery.

To ascertain the sex and size of the largest tiger I worked myself cautiously into the most frequented lair in order to examine a large, lone pine tree standing beside a trail far up on the mountain side. During this study I was attended by my cook, who had by this time developed into a successful and scientific tiger hunter. We covered each other as we clambered over the terraces worn bare by the inmates of the lair.

We found the pine tree marked as we had suspected, and slashed with fresh marks for a distance of eight feet or more, thus giving us something of an idea as to the immense size of the cat. Other trees were freshly marked, signifying both the presence and size of other animals. It now became necessary for us to use great caution around the monastery, as these same cats had been known to rush through an open door and attack people inside.

Tigers are continually on the move, so I decided to wait until one showed himself at some point within the great monastery bowl. This waiting was not of long duration. I was seated one day at noon with my family on the veranda of the monastery when the first outcry was heard from a settler's cottage across the creek, followed by shouting and screaming among the women and children.

Knowing a child had but a few days previously been carried away in just this fashion I grabbed my rifle and dashed off in the direction of the disturbance. Upon reaching the place I learned that nothing more serious than the stealing of a goat tethered in the dooryard had taken place. The frantic women of the home pleaded with me to pursue the tiger and retake the goat, declaring the flesh could be sold for several dollars.

I soon picked up the trail of the tiger, which was well defined in the tall ferns and grass. The fresh break led diagonally across the hill in the direction of the big lair. My hope was to overtake the animal feasting upon its kill in some of the tangle before it reached the lair and there have it out.

Following the trail for nearly half a mile I found that it passed into every clump of bushes even though it had to make slight detours in order to do so. At every one of these places I slowed up in order to make a careful survey before running into danger. This, of course, gave the animal a good lead, as he passed through this heavy cover much faster than I dared.

I was much disappointed upon finding that the cat did not halt in any of this cover, but proceeded right along until its trail entered a wide basin very densely covered with wild grape vines and sword grass. There was no question that the animal was in this depression devouring the goat.

Retracing my steps I organized a drive, assigning ten beaters, armed with pike poles and guns for defense and with gong and oil tins for creating a racket, to enter the basin from the side the tiger had entered it. I took my stand on an open ridge across which the animal would have to travel in order to reach the big lair.

The only position of any vantage I could find was behind a big bowlder over which the tiger would have to crawl if he followed what the beaters assured me was the only trail leading out of the basin. In taking this position it would be necessary for me to permit the tiger to reach the top of the bowlder not ten feet away before I could fire. Should I fail to drop the animal dead my only chance was to dodge behind and around the rock. It was an awkward and dangerous spot.

I had hardly taken my position when I heard the beaters shout that they had found the remains of the goat. I then heard the tiger bounding along the trail toward my hiding place. Peeking from behind the rock I could see the movements of the big cat as he approached to within twenty feet of the bowlder. Taking my position for a shot I waited breath-lessly for the animal to appear on the rock above me. He did not appear, so I suspected that he had seen me and was crouching on the opposite side, or possibly stealing around the base of the rock, making ready for a spring upon me.

It was now up to me to get onto the top of the bowlder, a thing I hurriedly, but with great caution, did. There was no tiger to be seen, but instead there was another trail branching off up the basin. I knew the tiger had followed this trail and would cross the ridge above me. There was nothing left for me but to beat him to the point where this trail crossed the ridge, as I knew it would, but without an idea as to precisely where. As I scrambled up the ridge as fast as I could I raised my head, only to see the animal emerge into the open a few rods ahead of me, stand for a second and then swing around until behind a pine tree. Then he began to stalk me. Reaching the base of the tree the brute laid his ears flat against his head and crouched for a spring. Just recall how your kitten used to look when about to spring upon a spool attached to the end of a string and you can appreciate what this animal looked like.

Quick work on my part was necessary, for the tiger, being above me, now had the vantage point. With perfect confidence I raised my rifle and fired square at the face of the crouching cat. To my surprise the animal whirled in the air and was gone. Upon investigation I found that my ball had struck the side of the pine tree behind which the animal was crouching, blowing out its side and scat-tering bark and splintered wood far and wide. I deplored the loss of such a trophy, but was quite reconciled by the fact that I had succeeded in turning a charge of the big cat into a hasty retreat at a time and under conditions when the odds were very much against me.

Later on reference will again be made to another appear-ance of this tiger when it will develop why the attack was diverted.

On the following afternoon I led a goat hard up against the lair of a tiger which had just killed a boy. Concealing myself behind a bank of ferns a short distance from the goat, I waited. Soon I saw the tiger emerge from dense cover. He came head on down the trail toward me until within easy attacking distance from the goat. As he paused for the attack I fired. Only the sportsman who has lost the opportunity of a lifetime can appreciate how I felt as I saw this huge wonderful trophy turn and bound into the lair, the second miss in two days.

After reflecting upon the situation for a few minutes I decided that my sights must be in error. So it proved the next day when I found that the front sight had been knocked over to an extent that deflected the ball thirteen inches to the right at the distance I had fired at either of these tigers. Some priest at the monastery had been looking at my gun and doubtless had given the sight a rap sufficiently hard to knock it well out of position. I had not detected this before going after the tiger. Possibly others having like experiences with the earlier make of Savage rifles had something to do with the searing on of the front sight, as is the case in all present-day makes of Savage high-power guns.

A few days later I responded to the appeals of some villagers and went after a tiger working havoc among the children and the herds. As luck would have it, I had become separated from my load carrier and so had but six cartridges with me when I connected up with the beast. Of course these cartridges were carried in the gun magazine.

Responding to the frantic calls of a traveler for help, I hurried along a trail, running right up on five tigers. Only one animal seemed to see me. This tiger hurriedly crouched as if for a charge, whereupon I fired. The big cat whirled a few times, showing it was hit, and then charged up the hill. I fired four more shots in rapid succession, the animal crumpling up at the last shot, going down with a blood-curdling howl which caused the other tigers to scatter.

My sixth shot was fired at a fine young male which was bounding into the high grass. At the report of the gun the tiger dropped in his tracks without a quiver.

Now I found myself in the awkward position of having an empty gun in hand and three tigers stalking around me. I lay concealed in the grass for more than half an hour, and until I was sure the tigers had moved out of the basin where my two dead trophies lay. I think I have never felt exactly as I did on that occasion.

While having my trophies carried from the hills it was with great difficulty that I restrained the villagers from setting upon them and beating their heads into a pulp. One old man came forward as the bearers were resting, and began to weep and lament over the recent loss of his cows, and proceeded forthwith to beat one of the tigers with a heavy hoe. Scarcely had he desisted from beating the animal when an old mother, supporting herself upon her staff, worked her way through the crowd of onlookers. She too began to weep and to wail, and then set upon one of the tigers with all her might, beating the animal and declaring it had almost broken up her home and carried away her only child.

A few days after I had fired at the tiger in the lair, striking the pine tree, the villagers of a near-by settlement located what seemed an especially daring animal. The community clairvoyant after consulting the idols in the temple declared he had a revelation from the "big ruler god" assuring success upon promise of the skin, if the villagers would go out and attack the tiger. Accordingly, more than one hundred men armed with pikes, poles, and guns loaded with rusty nails or slugs sallied forth for the attack. The onslaught lasted for more than half an hour, still the tiger seemed to have suffered but little. Finally several bold charges by the tiger materially cooled the ardor of the worshipers of the "big ruler god," whose frowning image was in the temple under the hill.

This crowd of enthusiasts had retired when a hunter, who was a member of our church in a neighboring village, arrived upon the scene armed with a very much repaired foreign-made double-barrel shotgun, loaded with slugs as long as the thumb and as round as the bore of the gun. He advanced to within twenty-five yards of the tiger before seeing it. He was followed by a number of friends bent upon seeing the execution. Two shots were fired at the tiger in rapid succession, one of which took effect. The wounded tiger roared and charged, whereupon the hunter fell limp and helpless in his tracks, being thus partly concealed by the growing potato vines of the field in which he stood.

The animal then charged the nearest man, who was standing upon a rise of ground overlooking an irrigation pool. The man plunged into the water, saving his life. The enraged beast then turned and charged at a third man standing upon a terrace below, passing clean over him and landing in the potato field within a few yards of the still helpless hunter. As the animal gathered itself for a spring upon this prostrate man it became exhausted and toppled over dead.

This animal was found to be blind in one eye, and to have a very deep flesh wound diagonally across the back. It proved to be the animal at which I had fired a few days before. The ball had expanded upon striking the tree, throwing fragments of wood into the face of the animal, while the jacket of the ball passed diagonally along the back, inflicting a very deep flesh wound. Thus ended the career of a tiger which had helped to fill the vacation days of one summer with a real kind of zest.

VI

Bluebeard of the Big Ravine

The first time that I ever heard of "Bluebeard," or "Black Devil," as the Chinese call him, was in the spring of 1910. The many stories I had previously heard of tigers and their doings had interested me but little, as I was busy and it seemed useless to entertain a thought of a real tiger hunt. But when I began to hear of the periodic visits of a "black tiger" I began to sit straight up and take notice. I desired, of course, not only actually to see, but to secure one of these peculiarly marked animals, the existence of which I could now no longer doubt.

In April I undertook for the first time to get a glimpse of this tiger, which had been moving about between the villages working havoc among both the cattle and the goats and most daring in attacking human beings. So mysterious indeed were the movements of this animal that many people declared it was some evil spirit abroad. The animal had been definitely reported as having been seen at points a considerable distance apart at about the same hour, so it was very much a question where I would be able to connect up with it.

I selected for my hunt the largest of a number of heavily wooded ravines, staking out a goat in what was known to be an oft-frequented lair. In doing this I had to take into account the man-eaters of the regular type known to be almost constantly found in and around this lair. When I actually started on the enterprise I realized that it was an undertaking well fitted to try the nerve of any man, for the only possible chance for a shot was to clear out a place with a jackknife where the goat could be tethered, and then conceal oneself in the grass to wait an attack.

Armed with a .303 Savage rifle I made an attempt to lure into my presence the wonderful tiger about which I had heard so many interesting stories. I did not meet with success this time, though I added to my experience that of having braved a tiger right in the lair under conditions rendering such an undertaking hazardous.

A couple of weeks later I decided to combine another hunt after this tiger with an evangelistic trip into the region adjacent to its habitat. Arranging with my burden-bearer to meet me on a certain day with supplies, and with my rifle, I set off on my quite extended itinerary, armed only with my shotgun, upon which I depended largely for supplying the larder with fresh meat. Arriving at the point on the day agreed upon, I found my burden-bearer had not turned up, so there was nothing for me to do but forego the pleasure of the attempt to get the prize upon which I had set my heart or else to undertake the task with a shotgun.

I had previously had an experience in shooting a tiger at a few yards' distance with a shotgun, so hesitated about going after this animal thus armed. But being very much pressed for time, I decided to make an attempt with the gun in hand. Some sticks of lead were molded by melting bird shot and pouring the metal into a small bamboo. These were cut into slugs and rolled quite round between flat stones. This furnished a formidable load. I then secured a goat and led it into the ravine, tying it at a point where two trails crossed. Taking my seat in the bushes a few yards from the goat, I settled down for a long wait, if this became necessary.

Long before the sun had set behind the rugged peaks overhanging the western rim of the ravine my attention was summoned by that mysterious something which the woodsman is unable to explain, but which directs the eye to a point where something has moved without the conscious realization of having seen it move. My eye was immediately fixed upon the object of my hunt— "Bluebeard," lying like a great domestic cat with head erect in a perfectly open place crossed by the trail.

The animal was all that had been pictured to me, and far more. Not to exceed twenty yards away, the great beast lay motionless, except for the nervous whipping of the end of the tail. I could easily have hit him with a pop-gun, yet I would not venture to fire with my shotgun, for I purposed not to send the animal wounded into the brush. In order to attack my goat the tiger would have to pass within eight yards of my hiding place, and it was my purpose to permit it to reach the nearest point before I fired.

Instead of attacking the goat as I had expected, the big cat slowly arose, sat for a moment in the trail, then stood erect for a few moments as if about to advance. But instead of doing so he turned around three times as if undecided what move next to make and showing signs of great nervousness, and then gracefully bounded up three terraces and disappeared behind the flowering wild pear bush. I waited almost breathlessly until dusk but the tiger did not appear again. I worked my way out of the ravine in the darkness with the satisfaction of having seen at short distance the trophy I was seeking, so that I could no longer doubt the actual existence of what seemed to be a new species of tiger.

A number of weeks elapsed before I could again devote any attention to "Bluebeard." It happened that on the eleventh of May I was passing through the same region when I was met by the villagers, who acquainted me with the sad news that a boy had been killed and eaten by a tiger the day before. I suspected the blue tiger, of course, and felt sure that he was then in the ravine where I had seen

him. Yielding to the entreaties of the villagers I decided
to spend the night in the community and try to get a shot.
Again I secured a goat and led it into the ravine, tethering it
in exactly the spot where the blue tiger had lain in the
trail.

After waiting in a cramped position for three hours
my cook, who was crouched beside me, nudged my elbow
whispering, "Tiger," and, glancing in the direction he was
looking, I saw a huge tiger watching the goat.

I was very much disappointed upon seeing that the
animal responding to the bleating of the goat was not the
blue trophy I so much desired. As I was now armed with
my rifle, one shot dropped the cat where it stood. I was,
of course, pleased over securing such a fine specimen,
but far from satisfied, as it was not the one upon which I
had set my heart.

In September of the same year I was again passing
through this region when I heard that the blue tiger had
rushed into a home the evening before and attacked a
child. The child had fallen asleep at its play under the
family table, around which were seated men smoking and
conversing. Everything was normal in the home when the
"Black Devil" rushed in at the open door and dashed at
the sleeping child. The Chinese declare the gods protected
the child, for instead of seizing the head of the child the
tiger grasped the leg of the table against which the head
was reclining, bolting out of the door with the table into
the open court. The child slept peacefully on until awak-
ened in the arms of its terrified mother.

Again I tried for the strange animal. This time I selected
a point on a ridge between two lairs, clearing away a few
yards with my pocketknife, in the center of which a goat
was tied. It was necessary to take our stand within ten
feet of the goat, as the cover was so dense. The unexpected happened, and the tiger approached along a path
from our rear.

Again my cook saw him first, calling my attention to what he declared was an animal. I glanced at the object, which appeared to me to be a man dressed in the conventional light blue garment and crouching as if picking herbs from beside the trail. I simply whispered to the cook "Man," and again turned my attention to watching the goat.

Again the cook tugged at my elbow, saying "Tiger, surely a tiger," and I once more looked at the object, this time to see what I thought was a man still upon his knees in the trail. I was about to turn again toward the goat when my cook excitedly said, "Look, look, it is a tiger," and, turning, saw the great beast lengthen out and move cautiously along the trail a couple of rods and then come to a sitting position near a clump of grass. Now focusing upon what I had altogether overlooked in my previous hurried glances I saw the huge head of the tiger above the blue which had appeared to me to be the clothes of a man. What I had been looking at was the chest and belly of the beast.

The tiger had followed a trail along the side of a hill, and I suppose was advancing in response to the bleating of our goat. I noiselessly turned around and sidled up to a little pine tree, leveling my rifle upon the chest of the brute.

As I was about to tighten my finger upon the trigger I noticed that the animal was interested in something below it and in the intervening ravine. Without removing the gun from the limb upon which it was resting I leaned forward to look into the ravine to see what was attracting the attention of the tiger. To my horror I saw two boys gathering up bundles of dry ferns and grass.

I dared not fire at the tiger. I would much rather never get a shot at him than to have him roll down wounded upon the defenseless boys. Instead of firing I stood up and moved so as to attract his attention. Upon seeing me

Bluebeard crouched low in the path behind the grass. I waited, moving back and forth so as to keep his attention directed my way, until the boys gathered up their fuel and moved out of danger.

The tiger crouched behind the tussock of grass motionless for half an hour. I suggested to my cook that the only chance to get a shot was to steal away and stalk him from the flank. This maneuvering required longer than we had anticipated, and when our heads came up over the level of the trail the tiger was gone. There were tracks in the trail showing where he had hurriedly retreated when we withdrew. Thus had come and gone the opportunity I had been waiting for through a full year.

I had met this strange tiger face to face and had deliberately permitted him to go at large, to continue his depredations throughout the neighborhood, but I felt quite satisfied in having seen so plainly and for so long a time the cat about which so many strange and almost uncanny tales had been told. The markings of the animal were marvelously beautiful. The ground color seemed to be a deep shade of maltese, changing into almost deep blue on the under parts. The stripes were well defined, and so far as I was able to make out similar to those on a tiger of the regular type.

The above notes were made several years ago. I moved away from this coast region in 1915, and with the exception of but two short visits have not been back since. I have thus not been able to make further first-hand studies of this wonderful animal, though many appeals have come to me far inland to return and devote some time to hunting this vicious man-eating member of the cat family.

While passing through the country with a party of travelers in 1920 the villagers all along the route declared that the so-called "Black Devils" had increased greatly in numbers, and were frequently seen. Eight days in succession one lay on an abandoned terrace during the afternoon just behind a village of eight hundred people. Practically everyone in this village told the same story, and described the tiger exactly the same, saying it was black with maltese markings, putting the thing just backward. Hunters say it appears black at a distance, but upon coming closer the lighter markings begin to show plainly.

This tiger, or tigers of this type, spread devastation among the peasant people during the latter part of 1921 and the spring of 1922. Seeing several accounts of the terrible toll of lives reported in the vernacular press in Foochow in April, 1922, with a description of the animal responsible for this killing, I decided to send my cook down to spend a month or so hunting him. The Chinese newspapers all referred to him as a "Blue Tiger," making me all the more anxious that my cook go after it, since I was unable to do so.

I instructed my cook to engage for the month a certain courageous hunter with whom I was acquainted. These two men soon connected up with the animal in the very midst of his man killing. In one community sixty people had been killed during the previous few weeks, one of them an especially good friend of mine. This man was digging ginger roots in his garden at the end of his house near the Rocking Stone Monastery when the tiger attacked, killing him and devouring him almost under the shadow of his own roof.

Careful inquiry was made among eyewitnesses concerning this tiger during this particular period of killing, and three hundred people who had seen the animal at least once at close quarters bore testimony as to markings, color, and size. One woman interviewed had a very narrow escape when she was crouched down at the foot of some stone steps washing clothes in a pool. The tiger lunged at her from above, passing completely over her and landing in the water. He then became terrified and instead of attacking again swam across the pool, clambering out on the other side with great difficulty. The woman was so frightened that she was unable to return to her home, a few yards away, until help came.

A very reliable hunter tells of having seen in April two of the dark-colored tigers together. He was stalking cock pheasants among the foothills when he heard a tiger call only a short distance away. Instead of trying to escape he concealed himself between two large bowlders having a crevice through which he could look in the direction of the tiger. Soon he saw a large blue tiger walk out of the cover and begin to paw the ground in an open space. This animal was in plain view, pawing and calling for near half an hour, when a second and smaller tiger of the same type walked into the open. The two huge cats stood for ten minutes in the open and then moved off diagonally down the hill and away from the concealed hunter. This man says the larger of the two would weigh more than four hundred and fifty pounds.

During the month of May my cook and his companion followed the animal for two weeks, during which time he hardly missed a day killing one or more persons. While the hunters were waiting in the vicinity of a kill of that day the tiger would move on a mile or so and kill another person. Thus the thing went on day after day until the tiger made the round of the big lair where I had first seen him, killing a man in the village where he had years before attacked the sleeping child, only to get a mouthful of table leg. Leaving this village he passed along a trail less than a hundred yards behind my cook's home, crossing a divide and killing two people.

The second hunter lived five miles from this point, and while he was assisting my cook in a hunt near this last kill, runners came from his own home, saying his three children had just been killed. Together they hurried to the home of the anxious hunter, to find the report true. The children had been playing happily in the dooryard when the tiger attacked, killing and carrying into the bush each of the three without anyone discovering it. Finally a neighbor woman noticed that the children were quiet and walked up beside their home to call them. She, too, was attacked and instantly killed. When the two hunters reached the place, they found the bodies of the woman and two of the children laying on an abandoned terrace behind the house, with the bones of an eleven-year-old girl less than four yards away.

My cook, Da Da, the man mentioned in Roy Chapman Andrews' *Camps and Trails in China*, and without exception the finest big game hunter to be found among the natives in South China, is set aside to devote a full year to hunting this tiger. With ten tigers to his credit already, I am confidently expecting that he will get one of the "Blue Cats" ere the year shall close.

VII

The Gentle Art of Tiger-Hunting

The method resorted to by many European sportsmen for hunting tigers in India would be impracticable in the mountainous regions of China. He who covets a shot at the big cat of China's wilds must be willing to forego such a vantage point as is afforded by a comfortable seat in a howdah on the back of a well-trained elephant.

There are three principal methods which are used by sportsmen in southern China when seeking a shot at one of these royal cats. Each of these has its advantages as well as disadvantages.

The method commonly used in some parts of taking a position in a tree near a recent kill and firing upon the beast as it returns is unsatisfactory and unsportsman-like. It is unsatisfactory because very uncertain, as the tiger more often never returns to a kill, and then, too, it is difficult in the region where I have studied tigers to find a tree in the right place. I did try the tree position on a few of my first hunts, but found the thing so unsatisfactory that I abandoned it. The only advantage is that the man behind the gun is absolutely out of danger.

Since so little has been reported from first-hand observation about the habits of tigers and certain other big game, a hunter should be actuated by more than a mere desire to secure a trophy, and should note down observations concerning the life history and movements of the animal. This has been the one impelling motive with me as I have carried the study of the tiger right into its lair, and has proven far more worth while than have the several fine specimens taken.

Cave shooting has been reported on by some sportsmen in the Amoy region, but I will have to pass this up as I have had no experience of the sort.

The second method tried by me is that of staking a goat out as a bait at some point either actually in, or hard up against a lair, and then concealing myself behind a blind of grass a short distance away to await an attack.

This method has the advantage of permitting the hunter to select his position, which is of vital importance after one has learned the mode of attack, for everything depends upon the relation of the position taken to the paths and trails along which the tiger is sure to travel. From a position of this kind I have repeatedly made long studies of the movements of tigers and their mode of attack at very short distances, and have had to correct many of the ideas I had held from childhood concerning the royal cat of the jungle.

I have never seen anything to bear out the contention made by some that a tiger always attacks a large animal from the rear by springing upon its neck and bearing it down. Several attacks which I watched made upon cows proved that the tiger attacks from the side and below, fastening its fangs in the neck in the region of the jugular vein, and, by placing the fore paws upon the chest, breaks the neck by a sudden wrenching of the head. Examination of a number of killed cows has proven in each case that the neck was broken.

In one instance noted a medium-sized tiger stalked a water buffalo and her yearling calf. The cow was in the terraced fields, standing in about six inches of water. She kept her body between the calf and the tiger as the latter moved around following the dykes trying to get an opportunity to attack. Finally the big cat did attack from the terrace above, springing upon the back of the cow, but I have always believed this was more by way of a ruse than with any thought of harming the cow. The tiger got the worst of it, however, for the cow humped up her back as the cat struck her, and by a quick flinching movement skidded the tiger off, landing it upon its back in the mud and water. The tiger crawled out to the nearest dyke and strode away, a mud-bespattered spectacle, but yet with all the dignity of its kind.

During the month of February, 1914, I had the pleasure of trying to give an officer of the Marine Corps, at the time an attaché to the American Legation in Peking, a shot at a tiger. This was Captain Thomas Holcomb, Jr., who proved to be one of the most courageous men I have had the pleasure of being out with. A streak of luck went against us on that afternoon, else my companion would have added one of the royal cats to his long list of trophies.

Together we had beaten out an oft-frequented lair in the forenoon with no results other than to satisfy ourselves that the tiger was not there, thus rendering it doubly certain that we would connect up in the big lair in the afternoon. It is always best to eliminate just as far as possible all the wooded ravines and suitable cover adjacent to a lair before actually taking one's stand, for in this way the chances of being surprised or flanked are reduced. On two occasions I almost lost my life by ignoring this practice, in both instances the tiger succeeding in approaching to within ten feet before I detected its presence.

In the afternoon we tethered a goat on a barren terrace after making a hurried survey of the possible approaches, and then withdrew fifteen yards to conceal ourselves behind a clump of bushes. Had we taken the precaution to build a blind, we would have gotten shots, but this was not done because I suspected we were so far in the lair as to be actually within a very few tens of yards of the tiger, so did not want to make any noise cutting or breaking branches to serve as a frame for the blind.

The first indication of the presence of a tiger was the alarm call of a certain little bird a few minutes from the time the goat began to call, and not to exceed fifty yards to our left. One of the things I early learned as a result of hunting in the lair was to make careful note of the call of certain birds. Learning to interpret their language was much to my advantage in locating the exact whereabouts of a moving tiger. Thus one can have sentries stationed on all sides who will sound the alarm just as soon as any animal of the cat family begins to stir. All such helps mean much where one is hunting an animal which moves with practically no sound.

We followed the approach of the tiger across our front along a faint trail to a wild pear bush, which soon became literally full of our feathered sentinels bristling with rage and scolding vigorously. The goat saw the tiger and lunged frantically at the tether-line. From the position now taken by the cat it could look right across beyond the goat and see us on an exposed side of the clump of bushes. Instead of charging, it crouched low, not exposing itself for a shot. My companion sat rigid and waiting for the charge.

As we both began to relax a little from the tension of the moment there was a sudden crash in the lair a little to our right. We both whirled in our positions expecting the onrush of a tiger from this direction. We could see the grass swaying under the weight of some heavy body. While our attention was centered upon this disturbance there was another crash near the pear bush, accompanied by the calls of a struggling deer. What had happened soon dawned upon both of us, so we rushed forward with the hope of overtaking the first tiger before it reached the deep tangle of the lair.

The animal was moving slowly over the terraces carrying a deer in its mouth. We were just a few yards behind, following as rapidly as we could over the terraces, up which we had to climb on all fours. We followed this tiger far into the lair, until we came to the well-defined tunnels through which we could only pass by crawling. With a feeling of keen disappointment we turned and quietly retreated to a safe position in the open.

What had happened is exactly what might be expected to happen under similar circumstances in a country where so much game abounds. The first tiger had stalked the goat to within easy attacking position, but had seen us and crouched low. A second tiger responded to the bleating of the goat and was approaching along the same line of terraces. A number of little deer came along on the next lower terrace, whereupon the tiger sprang upon one from above, crushing it down in the tall grass. The remaining deer ran back along the line of terraces into the very jaws of the other waiting tiger. This animal, too, made sure its strike, bringing down one of the muntjac. This tragedy was enacted within a few yards of us, and reflected very valuable light upon the study we were making of the habits of the wild tiger.

My companion that day will never forget the moment when two tigers were at work so near at hand. He was one of the leaders of the Marines on that memorable day when a handful of Americans threw the Germans back across the Marne in France, being one of two officers out of more than thirty who survived the three days' fighting. He wrote me later from Coblenz: "Caldwell, I will never forget the thrills of our tiger hunting in Fukien. It was great, but I say to you it cannot compare with the thrill connected with chasing the Hun."

On March 25, 1914, I was called upon to dispose of an exceedingly fierce and troublesome tiger. It was my plan to lure this beast into the open near its lair so as to make certain studies as well as get a shot, as this animal was noted for its daring attacks. Not being well acquainted with the lay of the land, I did not take into account one trail leading from the lair. Instead of emerging from its lair where I had figured it would, I saw it come out on a barren ridge within one hundred yards of me, where it paused and sat like a huge tom cat, probably making a survey of its surroundings before the final charge upon the goat. I leveled my gun for a shot, but with the sights used I found there was a blur in the twilight. There remained nothing for me to do but stalk the tiger before it got too dark for me to shoot with some degree of certainty.

As soon as I moved from my hiding the tiger crouched low. I could see that the eyes of the fierce beast were following me as I hurried forward into a depression which had to be crossed, changing my course a little, for I feared the tiger would flank me as I ascended the slope.

As my head appeared above the summit of the little knoll the tiger sprang to his feet. In order to get clear of some burned-over brush it was necessary for me to advance about twenty yards diagonally across the animal's front. While I was doing this the big cat was very nervous, switching its tail and throwing its ears back flat upon its head. I was expecting it to charge any second, yet it was necessary for me to withhold my fire until I was clear of all bushes, which brought me to within thirty yards of the animal, which was becoming very much worked up.

I saw the time had come to fire. Further delay might prove a serious matter. I was armed with the then most talked-of gun on the American market, a twenty-two Hi-power Savage rifle. The theorist had pronounced this ball too light to prove effective in big-game shooting, while, on the other side, guides in the Rockies had reported it as being effective on both bear and big-horn sheep. The discussion I had read pro and con in the sporting magazines concerning this gun confronted me as I. was brought to a place of severe test, but I dared not reflect long over these things.

I fired with great deliberation, covering as best I could my sights in the gloom, and striking the animal squarely back of the ribs. It was far too dark to undertake to pick any vital spot. The big cat lunged into the air, coming down dead. The ball entered the stomach cavity, doing terrible execution. Had the animal swallowed an explosive bomb the results could not have been more disastrous. No animal could sustain such a shock and live to do much damage.

Two observations worth mentioning were noted during the study of this tiger. It was most interesting to notice that when a tiger runs down hill it is no longer the slender, agile and graceful cat known to everyone who has visited a zoo. When making a rapid descent a tiger resembles very much a cow going down a steep place. The back is very much humped, and the body drawn up to not much more than half its ordinary length. This is in keeping with what I had always been advised by Chinese hunters, who have said that I should retreat downhill if attacked by a tiger, since the front legs were so much shorter than the hind as to cause it to travel with great difficulty down a steep grade.

Another observation was not altogether in keeping with what I had gathered out of my earlier reading about the big jungle cat. I found the stomach of this animal filled with recently devoured food, among which was a dog which had been eaten but a very short time. Instead of withdrawing to the seclusion of a quiet lair and sleeping for a full day, this animal attacked with all the vigor of a ravenously hungry one, when the facts are that it could not possibly have eaten the goat had it secured it. A tiger doubtless kills because it is its instinct to kill.

The remaining, and by far most interesting, method of hunting tigers is the so-called "still-hunt." This is the most interesting method because it reveals to the observant sportsman much concerning the home life of the tiger otherwise difficult to learn. There are rich rewards for the man who will enter the lair of a tiger with the purpose of not only finding the inmate of the home, but with a desire to make as many observations as possible which will throw light upon the domestic habits of this royal cat.

It is needless to say that still hunting is attended with many real dangers not encountered in any other method of tiger hunting. Many are the times a sound, greatly magnified by the tension of the moment, brings one to a sudden standstill with the heart pounding away well up in the throat. One often halts for a moment with attention centered upon some interesting find, when an imaginary tiger is detected stealing up under cover from the rear. While trying to locate what you now feel is certainly hiding in the bush close at hand, as the awful silence of the wilds bears down with tremendous force it is almost next to impossible to keep from breaking wildly away through the lair.

I shall never forget the struggle I have repeatedly had with that imaginary tiger which has cost me so much cold fear. Any man would rather meet all the flesh-and-blood cats in tigerdom in the open than be forced to endure that spell which sometimes comes over one when he feels himself alone in the lair of a tiger.

This is the price almost any man will have to pay for his initiation into the sport of still hunting in a tiger's lair. But all this soon passes away when one becomes hardened to the presence of both real and imaginary tigers, the silence of the wilds and all else, and really finds himself enjoying this stealing around from apartment to apartment of the lair, often connected by well-defined tunnels through which he must get down upon hands and knees and crawl for a long distance.

The most nerve-racking experience I have ever had in a tiger's lair was when I foolishly entered the lair of a tigress with three small kittens, one of which had been captured by some wood choppers the day before. The mother cat in her grief and anger had clawed great holes in the ground and attacked trees, which she had gnawed to shreds as high as she could reach. No human maniac could have torn things up any more than that enraged tigress had.

I found the remains of a pangolin which had been torn to bits and scattered about. The only thing that saved me probably from just such a fate was the fact that the lady of the place had given up hope of finding her lost child and had moved out with her remaining two.

Notwithstanding there are many real dangers attending still-hunting for tigers in the tangle of their lair, still one feels richly repaid and rewarded for the risk he has run when he begins to sum up his observations. One of the most interesting finds as a result of an hour's prowling around in an oft-frequented lair is concerning the food of the cat. There are evidences a-plenty that a tiger carries its kill from long distances to devour it upon one certain terrace, or "dining table."

A sad thing happened on the 14th of April, 1914, which illustrates this point. The remains of a fifteen-year-old boy were found in a large grave in a lair but a few miles from Futsing City. No child had been reported missing in the neighborhood. Everything indicated that the child had been brought alive from a distance to this lair, as the sides of the grave were besmeared with fresh blood of the victim, indicating that the tiger had tortured the boy just as a cat tortures and plays with a mouse so long as there is life in it.

One will find on the favorite terraces the remains of prey which have been brought in. A fresh kill of a medium-sized animal shows plainly how the tiger first uses its rasplike tongue for removing most of the hair before devouring the flesh. The hair will be found in a circle around what remains of the kill.

While there is nothing to indicate that a tiger always brings its prey to one place to eat it, still there is much that would prove that this is frequently done. On a terrace of the kind one will find the skulls and bones of deer, wild hog, dog, pig, porcupine and pangolin, as well as other domestic and wild animals. The Chinese often raid a lair in order to pick up the bony scales of the pangolin, which are highly prized for medicinal properties. In addition to the larger animals, frogs, reptiles, and the like are taken when opportunity affords.

On the night of April 22, 1914, a party of frog hunters were returning from a hunt. A man carrying a sack of frogs was attacked and killed by a tiger. No attempt was made to drag the man away. It would appear that the animal was attracted by the croaking of the frogs in the sack, as it was ripped and much torn.

It is beside some trail or path in a lair where one finds the trees "marked." This is one of the first signs an experienced tiger hunter will look for. Catlike, the tiger measures its full length upon the tree. The sign is doubly interesting to sportsmen, for it serves not only the purpose of assurance of the presence of a tiger, but it gives a fair idea as to the reach of the animal as well.

One will invariably find the trails leading from a lair marked also. So frequently is this done that one would be led to suspect it is for the same purpose that a dog marks the road traveled. In this operation the tiger brushes away the grass and leaves beside the trail, and, while considerable strength must be used, the claw prints never appear. The full size of the padded foot is apparent. The way in which the debris is gathered in a heap shows plainly that the stroke is with the fore paw.

There are many more observations that reflect light upon the domestic life of a tiger which are reserved for the man who will venture to enter the lair and seek for signs which experience helps to interpret. The Chinese have had it handed down for ages that a tigress never has more than two kittens of her own kind, the third always being a leopard. It was with difficulty that I convinced the man accompanying me upon one trip, when we found a tigress with four kittens, that the handsome beast was the mother of the four.

I have learned much by studying the habits of tigers in their native habitat in China, but those observations which reflected the greatest degree of light upon the real life of the royal cat have been the results of prowling around on a still hunt in the lair.

Plate 5
The recorded world's record Big Horn (*Ovis comosa*), killed by the
author in November, 1919, in Shansi Province, China.

Plate 6
A haul from which we were to select a Christmas dinner. Everyone
concerned drew hog, and an after-dinner vote decided it the best
meat ever eaten.

Plate 7

1. At times the trackers are hundreds of yards, and even half a mile or more, ahead. In time of great danger the crew from the second boat—for they always travel in pairs—hurries forward to the assistance of those calling loudly upon Ma Chu for help.

2. It is when the tow-line snaps, leaving only three men on hoard, that wrecks most often occur. The momentum of the boat causes it to stand still for several seconds in the strongest rapids after the tow-line has been severed, often allowing the man directing the placing of the line, whose position is always far back, to gather the severed end of the line and make it fast around a rock before the boat actually begins to drift.

3. The little "rice boat" which has carried me thousands of miles over the rapids with but one mishap, when the bottom was caved in by a submerged rock while shooting a rapid. The bunting at the stern carries one anywhere in this bandit-infested area in perfect safety.

4. What you see piled upon the flat rocks is rice, which has been carried there by the farmers and spread out to dry. At night, or during a storm, the grain is swept into piles and protected by straw-mat coverings.

Plate 8

1. Power is harnessed by merely lowering the crude wheel in the current. This mill works equally well in all stages of the river.

2. Certain gods seem to like a home in the top of some inaccessible peak. The daring devotee scales these heights to offer sacrifice, pasting bits of Joss paper on the small ledges which serve as stepping-stones for ascending the heights.

3. Both birds and gamblers seek the good office of the gods supposed to roost in the branches of the sacred Banyan tree.

4. Pedestrians after ascending several thousand feet, pass a stone upon a pile on the divide, signifying both allegiance and gratitude to the hill-god or genii, which might be nothing more than the spirit of some deified animal.

VIII

My Friend the Serow

To describe accurately and place definitely the serow is a very difficult undertaking, although it is one of the most interesting of the big game of China. Fewer European sportsmen have shot serow than any other of the big-game group, with the probable exception of the *takin*, which is a very closely allied species. A careful study of the living animal is attended with very great difficulties and is exceedingly hazardous, as the animal is only found upon almost inaccessible cliffs and precipices of the high-altitude mountains. Consequently, serow-hunting is as strenuous sport as can be conceived, but the trophy is well worth the price one pays, for there are but few prizes to be taken in China that can give the sportsman a greater degree of satisfaction than a well-maned serow buck. Both wapiti and big-horn hunting are child's play as compared with serowhunting in southern China.

Scientifically speaking, serow are an offshoot of the *Bovidæ*, and very probably a member of the subfamily *Rupicaprinæ*. They seem to occupy an intermediate position between the true goat and the antelope. The horns of both sexes are about the same in shape and size, being very beautifully ringed and rigid, and tapering to a very sharp and dangerous point. So far as I have been able to carry out the study of the horns of the sexes in something like a score or more specimens, I have found those of the female a trifle closer together, though this may not hold as a characteristic difference between the male and the female.

When cornered or brought to bay on a cliff a serow puts up a most terrific fight, ripping dogs viciously with the horns, dashing them lifeless to the depth below. It unhesitatingly attacks man when cornered.

The forms found in the mountains of Japan, China, and India differ considerably in shading and color of mane. The form found in Chekiang and Fukien provinces is the white-maned form, and is very likely *Capricornis samatrensis argyrochartes*. This is one of the largest forms. I have taken full-grown males weighing more than three hundred pounds, and one female but a trifle, if any, smaller.

On one occasion while hunting in Chekiang province I saw one fine specimen with a rich, brown mane. Whether or not this represents a second form in south China cannot yet be determined.

The color of the China type of serow is a very dark to almost black coat of long coarse hair upon a heavy coat of short light-colored hair. The lower legs are rusty red to almost fox brown. The mane is white, extending well down the back, but heaviest on the neck.

The feet of this goat-antelope are well fitted for cliff climbing. In fact, the animal is so agile upon precipices as to cause a saying among Chinese hunters that the serow's feet are supplied with a secretion of gluelike substance which prevents it from either slipping or falling. I suppose the goral is the only member of the allied family which can compare with the serow as a cliff roamer.

Though I have enjoyed some great sport hunting serow on the cliffs not far from Yenping, Fukien, and have had opportunity for careful study of the animal in its native habitat and at close range in these mountains as perhaps few white men have anywhere, still my most interesting experiences while serow-hunting were in Chekiang Province in September, 1919, when conducting a small expedition especially for specimens of this interesting form, under the auspices of the American Museum of Natural History of New York.

I was asked to devote as much as four weeks if necessary in this immediate region in order to secure representative specimens of the Chekiang serow. I invited a friend, J. H. Snoke, M.D., of Shanghai, who had hunted tigers with me in Fukien, to accompany me on this difficult and uncertain quest. We reached the town of Tung-lu, sixty miles inland from Hangchow, where we were taken in hand by the Rev. H. Castle, who probably is the most experienced serow hunter in China, and to whom is due all the credit for our highly successful trip.

Leaving Tung-lu we traveled twenty miles up a small creek right into the heart of the mountains. The weather was still intensely hot and the foliage still heavy on the trees and underbrush, both conditions rendering hunting extremely difficult, but I had become so accustomed to both that the prospects did not worry me at all.

Arriving at the village of Yaw late in the afternoon, we were met by an old scout who had selected seven chosen men to act as beaters. At any season of the year when the foliage is heavy on the low brush and tangle of vines clinging to the ledges of rocks it is next to useless to undertake to secure serow by the still-hunting method. The only sure way of getting the animals on the move is by sending in beaters who shout and beat the brush, rolling rocks down the cliffs. This method is almost certain to get the animals on the move, when from some distant vantage point a shot is possible. Much of the shooting is necessarily at long range and while the animal is racing across some open space. All the conditions attending hunting serow, so far as my experience goes, are such as to make one feel proud over taking a trophy.

When the old guide called upon us, bringing his beaters, we went as far as possible into the details of the proposed hunt for the following day. But do what he could, our friend Castle was unable to get the old scout to divulge even the direction he would take us. In a hushed tone he assured us the genii of the mountains, known as "The Booster of the Hills," would warn all the serow of our plans to invade their sanctuary, and they would all scurry far back into the range and hide themselves in the home of this god.

To insure an early start in the morning we invited the old hunter and his men to come to our boat for breakfast. This plan proved highly successful, for an hour before the crack of dawn these men were standing lined up on the shore waiting for the gang plank. Each hunter was armed with a sickle for cutting his way through the tangle, and a primitive gun which would doubly insure him a share of any animal taken by any man in the party.

There is an unwritten law among the hunters to the effect that the man actually killing the animal is entitled to the head and skin in recognition of his prowess, the additional parts being equally distributed between the hunters and beaters. I recall one time when I went out to secure a muntjac to divide among the missionaries of my station for Christmas. There were fourteen hunters and hangers-on when the first drive began. Within ten minutes I put up a little deer myself, knocking it right over. This was exactly what I wanted, but in order to get the animal I had walked up and killed I had to purchase for cash fourteen-fifteenths of the flesh at twenty-five cents per pound.

Our hunters became restless to get away as dawn was breaking over the distant crags. When all was in readiness the guide simply waved his long arm toward the rising sun and broke off in silence across the plain. The time had not yet come when it was wise to speak above a whisper suggesting the exact locality we were to visit. The "Booster" was still abroad and would not retire to his cave or cranny until the bats went to rest, a few of which could yet be seen feeding along the stream bed.

Within two hours from the time we left our boat we were standing upon the first saddle of the mountains, three thousand feet above the plain. It had been a stiff climb, during which the hunters never suggested a halt or rest. High peaks and rugged crags were on all sides of us with no escape other than a trail leading into the valley on the opposite side.

Here the scout halted and for the first time announced where we would hunt, pointing out the face of a cliff three miles up the range. To reach this hunting ground the climb was even more strenuous than the one we had left behind, as we had literally to burrow our way through the dense brush and tangle. The heat was intense on account of the humidity, and the forenoon sun was beating down upon us with tremendous power.

In due time we stood at the foot of the cliff from whence we could look far down the divide upon which we had stood near two hours earlier. The going through the brush had been slow and tiring. Not being supplied with canteens we were almost famished for water, so we made a detour in order to get a drink before entering upon the hunt proper. Only those who have been through the ordeal can begin to appreciate what it means to be without water in a land like China.

As we climbed further in order to get our positions, Mr. Castle pointed out place after place where he had routed serow, killing one here and another there, but still the old guide broke trail and led us on into the deeper, wilder regions. Finally halting under a wind-blasted pine, the hunter heaved a long sigh, pointing at the rugged cliff, saying, "There is where we get our first serow."

After consultation with the hunters, Mr. Castle pointed out our various stations, asking me if I could possibly work my way around to a jagged point breaking off like a

great wedge driven deep into the side of the range. I
scrambled away over some very rough territory, allowing
myself fifteen minutes to reach the point before the drive
should begin.

Before I had reached my station the beaters began to
shout and roll huge rocks down the cliff. I clambered over
a precipice, beyond which was the stand I had agreed to
take. From the foot of the cliff, and not twenty feet below
me, dashed two large serow, stopping under a little cover
less than two rods away from whence they bombarded
me with hisses and snorts. I dared not halt for a shot lest
I fail to carry out my part of the program. Before I reached
the bottom of this cliff I heard one of the beaters fire his
gun and raise a loud shout.

Though much out of breath when I reached my station I
was greatly joyed to hear the beaters announce that the
animal was leading in my direction. The course taken
would bring it out on the point at or just above the practically barren cliff over which I had just climbed.

While I was trying to compose myself for a sure shot I
heard the brush cracking and crashing under the weight
of a heavy body. Suddenly the huge buck emerged from
the dense cover and dashed across the face of the cliff.
The animal had chosen a perfectly safe runway, had I
been stationed on the point above the cliff, but as it was
I had a fair view of it from the time it broke cover. It
resembled more a donkey than any animal of the wilds
that I had ever seen. Its white mane was bright in the
sunlight. The horns so closely in line with the ears gave
the head the appearance of that of a mule.

As the animal reached the open I raised my untried
250-3000 Savage and fired at the shoulder. One shot was
all that was necessary, as the animal collapsed in a heap
in the brush at the opposite side of the cliff.

I said nothing to anyone about the kill, knowing that
such an announcement would frustrate any further drive.

Half an hour later, therefore, when I did call out that I had killed a serow none of the hunters believed me. They had seen sportsmen become hysterical upon killing such a trophy, and could not believe me when I announced that I had shot a fine buck. It was not until I had dragged one of the hunters by force to the dead animal that I could get him to believe that I had done anything but fired and missed. When he saw the animal dead before him, he only grunted and said, "What did you keep still about it so long for?"

On the following day we again scaled the cliffs for another drive, but six of the hunters deserted us at noon on account of the intense heat, just at a time when a buck was snorting at us from across a ravine. Even the best Chinese hunters are exasperating at times, not being willing to endure the Fatigue necessary to insure a successful drive. And, too, not understanding the strategy of a hunt, and totally ignoring the matter of direction of the wind, they often render fruitless an otherwise successful hunt.

The signs observed during this second day indicated a rutting season and habits much like those of the common deer of eastern United States. I found great patches of newly pawed earth, as well as many trees and shrubs badly horned.

On Monday morning we were astir at an early hour as a result of the day of rest and relaxation. We attacked the almost perpendicular face of the range at daylight, but it was nearly nine o'clock when we stood upon the top of the divide discussing positions and the drive. Suddenly and without warning a fine buck broke cover and started across the face of a cliff with the grace of a fawn frisking on a lawn. Well-directed shots by Doctor Snoke brought this animal down. One could but wonder how any animal could possibly keep its footing upon such a steep and rugged cliff.

We started two more serow in the next ravine but did not succeed in getting either, as the tangle was too much

for us. On account of a change of plans, which now allowed
me but a few days to get back to Shanghai and ready to
start north to join Roy Chapman Andrews in Peking for
an expedition along the Mongolian frontier, we were compelled to cut our serow hunt short. With two fine specimens
as a result of three days' hunting we felt well repaid for
the trip.

Serow-hunting in Fukien is even more difficult than
that I experienced in Chekiang. There are a great many
of these animals in the mountains around Yenping, where
I have succeeded in securing a fine series for the American
Museum of Natural History. Serow-hunting has a fasci-
nation about it all of its own, doubtless partly due to the
difficulties attending the sport, but the trophy is well
worth winning.

IX

Stalking the Big Horn

Accepting the theory of the scientist that the so-called American elk and the big horn crossed the ice, or at one time narrow neck of land now known as the Bering Strait, we must conclude that the sheep have degenerated considerably, for the big horn of the American continent are but pigmies as compared with their progenitors in Asia. The elk, however, compares favorably in size and magnificence with any specimen recorded from either Manchuria, Siberia, or northern China.

In trying to arrive at something like an accurate comparison between either the wapiti or sheep of Central Asia with the so-called elk of the American continent (*Cervus canadensis*), or the big horn (*Ovis canadensis*), it must be borne in mind that not more than a few tens of the former have ever been measured and reported on, while in the case of the latter it is safe to say that a maximum measurement has in all probability been recorded.

There are in Central Asia five quite distinct types of sheep recorded, with fair chances that other will yet be added. *Ovis poli* is a remarkably fine animal found in the high-steppe region of Central Asia, and is named after Marco Polo, who is credited with having discovered it. This species is characterized by the great length and wide spread of horns. The record measurements, in so far as I have ever noted, are:

Length of horn, 76 inches.
Basil circumference of horn, 16 2/3 inches.
Height of animal at shoulders, 46 inches.
Measurements are of specimens in British
Museum, as reported.

Possibly the largest sheep thus far recorded is found
in the Alti Mountains. This animal has been much hunted
by European sportsmen, who have considered it one of
the most coveted of all trophies. Notwithstanding the efforts
put forth to secure trophies of this magnificent animal,
comparatively speaking, but few have ever been taken.
This sheep is known as *Ovis littledalei*. The recorded
measurements are:

Length of horn, 62 1/2 inches.
Basil circumference of horn, 18 1/2 inches.
No record as to height at shoulder of this
specimen.

The Tibetan sheep is characterized by the massiveness
of its horns. Long horns or rather wide reach are the exception in this species, as the animal keeps the points worn
off in order to be able to feed freely upon the short grass.
This sheep is known as *Ovis hodsoni*. Measurements are:

Length of horn, 75 inches.
Basil circumference of horn, 18 1/2 inches.
Height at shoulder estimated at 48 inches.

The species most common to Mongolia and Siberia is
Ovis ammon, and is called by the Monguls the Argili. Possibly a greater number of this species than of any other
have been taken by European sportsmen. The recorded
measurements thus far are:

Length of horn, 62 inches.
Basil circumference of horn, 19 inches.
Approximate height at shoulder, 48 inches.

This entire group comprise trophies over which sportsmen have all but gone insane. There is no animal hunted which is more wary and difficult to take than the big horn of Central Asia. The North China species, *Ovis comosa*, sometimes confused with *Ovis ammon*, is one of the finest of the entire sheep group thus far recorded. I killed the world's record of this species in November, 1919, in the mountains of northern Shansi Province, hard up against the Mongolian border.

Up to this time the record had been reported on by the noted scientist, Arthur de C. Sowerby, in this same region. The skull with horns attached had been picked up, the animal very likely having been killed by wolves. The horn measurements at the base were nineteen and one half inches in circumference. It must be remembered, however, that this measurement was of dry horns, which would mean the actual measurements in life were approximately the same as that of my trophy when killed, which had nineteen and three quarter inches basil circumference.

I saw fossil skulls taken from the bed of the Feng Ho River in Shansi Province which far exceeded any records for present-day trophies recorded. The fine animals now found upon these rugged mountains serve to show something of what once existed in the region when the big horns were at the zenith of their glory.

The area where the sheep are now found in China comprises a very limited region of most rugged mountains. The big horns were reported as early as 1876, when a number of heads were taken by European sportsmen. After this there elapsed a period of years when they were practically forgotten, thus escaping destruction other than at the hands of the Mongol hunters armed with primitive weapons. In recent years there has been a decided revival of interest in this wonderful but rapidly disappearing trophy, possibly a greater number being taken by European sportsmen during the past decade, or a little more, than during all previous time.

In the fall of 1919 I was granted a few months off by the Board of Foreign Missions of my church for the purpose of joining Roy Chapman Andrews in an expedition along the Mongolian border to secure a complete series of this sheep, *Ovis comosa*, which is rapidly approaching extinction.

After a short but successful expedition into Chekiang Province hunting serow, I hurried north to join Mr. Andrews in Peking, upon his return from a long and hard summer's expedition in Mongolia. This outing was a much appreciated respite for me before plunging into the routine of work at my station in southern China, for I had been spending two busy years in the homeland in connection with a special missionary campaign.

Just the outfitting and packing for an expedition of this kind seemed a big undertaking to me, but Andrews seemed to know just what he wanted, and what quantity of each article, so that we got through the task in a remarkably short time.

Leaving Peking, we traveled by rail to Kalgan and beyond on a Chinese built and operated railroad. The rolling stock was American, but the road had been conceived and executed by Chinese engineers, and it was a credit to its builders. I doubt whether I ever enjoyed a day's train travel as I did that day over a route made famous by the Mongol chiefs, who led many an attack upon the Chinese over this same way. At intervals during the whole day we could get glimpses of the Great Wall which for so many centuries preserved China from being completely overrun by the invader.

Reaching what was then the railhead at nine o'clock in the evening we found some difficulty in getting all our belongings transferred to an inn on account of a rain-storm. In this work we were greatly assisted by the station agent, a young man of strong Christian character, who spoke English fluently.

Traveling in almost any part of China to-day one learns to appreciate men who are the product of Christian missionary work. Whether or not professing Christians themselves, their actions and general bearing reflect credit upon Christian education. There are, of course, exceptions to this as to any rule, but one who has traveled much in unfrequented parts of China will bear testimony to the real worth of Christian missionary work as manifested through the lives and character of many men he meets.

We were delayed a day in Fengcheng on account of the difficulty experienced in securing the necessary horses and cart for the long trip across the province. It finally proved necessary to buy outright three horses for saddle purposes, hoping to be able to dispose of them at a reasonable price upon our return. The way this deal ended, however, suggested that we were better hunters than horse-traders, for we practically had to give the animals away upon our return, although they were in as good or better condition than when we purchased them.

The trip across Shansi Province kept us constantly alert. I walked considerably after the first day, as I had not ridden a horse for about twenty years, and one day was enough to satisfy me for the time being.

While walking along beside the cart road we had great sport collecting a very beautiful little sand rat known as gerbil (*Meriones auceps*). These little long-tailed rats abound in colonies in the sand dunes and sandy wastes where it was possible by careful stalking and more careful shooting to secure specimens each day sufficient to keep the taxidermists working until a late hour each night in the inns where we put up.

I very much wanted to get both bustard and antelope, which abound on the Shansi plains, but was unfortunate in not connecting up with either. At Lake Tai Hai we had wonderful duck and goose shooting.

This lake is one of the wonders of the trip across the province. It may well be called the sportsman's paradise so far as hunting water fowl is concerned. During the period of migration literally tens of thousands of shore birds, ducks, geese and swans gather there, offering wonderful shooting. The railroad has long since been constructed to far beyond this lake, so that it is a simple matter for sportsmen from Peking to run up there for a weekend shoot.

We spent one night at this lake, stocking our larder with fresh meat during a few hours' sport early in the morning.

As we neared the great Kweihuacheng plain Mr. Andrews began to school me in the matter of estimating distances, for the success or failure of a hunt after the big horn may rest upon this very fact. This thing is not nearly so true now, however, where a person is using one of the modern high-power rifles, as it was a few years ago when the ordinary gun was used, though I did make some miserable misses while shooting at the first herd of sheep because I had not fully grasped what my teacher was trying to get into my thinking all along the way.

I walked upon a group of eight sheep the second day out, and could have easily secured a trophy had I reckoned at all accurately as to distance. As it was, I was firing point blank at the sheep at more than seven hundred yards, supposing them to be not to exceed half that distance. The atmosphere is so clear and rarified that things stand out much magnified, rendering the calculating of distances exceedingly difficult for the one who for the first time undertakes to shoot under such conditions.

When I returned to camp at the end of the second day out, reporting that I had seen sheep at three points, I supposed that, of course, our guides would again head that way the following morning. I never could quite figure out just why they did not, but instead broke off to the left and toward what appeared to be an absolutely inaccessible cliff two thousand feet or more high. Lame and stiff from the climbing of the previous day, I was in no shape to attack such a climb, and was feeling the weight of my feet terribly when some one of the party directed our attention to a huge sentinel ram standing on the very highest crag as still and rigid as some molten image.

It was a wonderful sight, and just what I needed to make me forget aching limbs, heavy feet, and all else. We all lay down on the slope and watched the lone ram for nearly a quarter of an hour. He squared around and surveyed the horizon in one direction, and then in another, seeming all the time to be looking far over our heads. There was in all his actions but one which suggested that he possibly saw us. That was when he disappeared from view as if satisfied with his survey for friends or foe, only to hurry back to his pinnacle point for a second and then a third look. He must have taken a final peep later and after we had begun to hurry up the slope, for when we reached the top the old ram was nowhere to be seen. We followed for a long way down a ridge fresh tracks which showed that the sentinel had hurried to cross the creek at the bottom of the deep ravine only to enter the labyrinth of rugged mountains on the opposite side.

Possibly our guides had in mind connecting up with this giant sheep somewhere back in this wild when they suggested that we separate for the day's hunt, but of this they never spoke, my hunter simply tugging at my elbow and pointing to the depths of a dark and icy ravine leading into the very heart of the range. The other guide motioned Mr. Andrews to follow him up what seemed to be an impossible climb.

I am not sure which of us would have had the more difficult day if it had been necessary for me to climb out of the head of this ravine to either of the divides. As it was, I had a very easy and happy day, returning to camp by the middle of the afternoon with my first big trophy, while poor Andrews did not stagger in until after nine o'clock in the evening, and then nearly dead, as he had helped his hunter over miles of mountain with a burden of two heads and skins.

Soon after separating from Mr. Andrews I found myself following along a frozen stream bed, everywhere blocked by jumbled masses of stone. Walking was exceedingly difficult and dangerous, as the rocks were covered with a glaze of ice. We had to move so slowly that I was really suffering with the chill which seemed to penetrate into the very marrow.

My guide was not hunting, his every action showing he was merely working his way up this gulch in order finally to come out upon the top of the range. I saw far ahead of us a patch of wedge-shaped sunlight which fell across the ravine, and I hurried along to reach it, hoping to be able to thaw out a bit. Just as we entered this area of sunshine I raised my head to see what formation of peaks would cast such a symmetrical shadow in this deep ravine, only to see four sheep leisurely moving along toward a saddle in the range.

I did not spend much time calculating distances, for I felt sure that these animals were safely within the five-hundred-yard range. Dropping upon one knee I raised my gun to fire at the largest sheep, which was at this time nearest the divide. To my disgust I found I could not so much as see the mountain through my sights, to say nothing of seeing sheep. The reflection from the copper front peep sight produced great spokes of light wholly obliterating everything.

I shifted my position in order to get a shot, whereupon the big ram stood looking at me, letting the ewe and two other rams pass him. When I tried for a second time to get a shot the ewe stood upon the skyline while the other sheep moved slowly forward. Again it was impossible to shoot.

I now became almost frantic lest these sheep should slip away before I could get to the shadow on the other side of the light wedge. Hurrying as much as I dared, lest I attract the attention of the rams and send them bounding over the divide, I moved forward to within a few yards of the shadow of one of the twin peaks, whereupon I lunged forward, crouching low so as to be in the shadow and hurriedly fired at the big ram now nearing the skyline.

At the report of the gun he leaped high in the air. His feet had hardly touched earth when I fired a second shot, and while he staggered I fired the third. The big sheep crumpled and lunged forward, disappearing in a depression.

I knew that the sheep was down, for another ram stopped on the skyline and looked long in the direction of his leader, offering me a very fine shot. One sheep is enough to try to handle alone in such a place, so I refrained from shooting at the second ram, which carried a magnificent head.

My guide and I clambered and scrambled up the mountain, having to make a wide detour on account of the almost perpendicular face of the slope. From a distance I saw the huge gray body of the ram lying upon the steep side of the basin.

Upon reaching the animal I was amazed at its immense size, length of body, and massiveness of limbs. As I admired all these my guide went wild with excitement, mercilessly mauling me over the back and hauling me around that I might look at the head. I could only catch now and then the words, "They do not grow larger horns than these," as the almost hysterical Mongol pranced first around me and then around the sheep.

After I got him sufficiently quieted down I took his picture beside the ram. He then beat me over the back shouting, "They do not grow bigger."

While I was studying my trophy and waiting for better sunlight that I might expose another roll of films the eagle eye of my guide saw somewhere in the distance and far above us Mr. Andrews and his hunter, to whom he shouted the news that I had killed a very large sheep. I shouted off in the same direction to Mr. Andrews that I had killed a sheep which certainly was a beauty.

This was one of the supreme hours of my life, for I had traveled from New York to Mongolia for the purpose of assisting Mr. Andrews in securing a series of these sheep. I had heard several applications for a place on this expedition turned down flatly, and I had heard Andrews say with considerable confidence that the two of us could secure the trophies desired. It was a great relief to me, after the experience of the previous day, to have killed a sheep large enough to excite my guide as this one had.

I had fired three shots at this animal in about as rapid succession as it is possible for a Savage rifle to work, from a most awkward position, making a triangle of holes just back of the foreleg which could be covered with the palm of my hand. Any one of the shots would have finished the animal off. I could now breathe easy in the satisfaction of having actually secured that for which I had traveled so far, yet little appreciating the real magnificence of the trophy.

It is a task to be remembered to skin out such a specimen alone, or with such help as the guide can offer, but we got through in good time and started for camp just four hours after I had killed the sheep. The husky Mongol staggered under his load of head and skin, which he said weighed nearly 150 pounds.

Late in the evening Mr. Andrews came into camp with one large head and that of a small ram, both of which fitted right into the series of seven heads selected for the life group, showing beautifully the horn growth. Later we both secured additional heads, but nothing rivaling the massive head of my first ram. Three of the heads taken compare favorably with any ever taken out of that North Shansi region.

I have never learned of any part of the sheep being especially valuable for medicinal purposes, as is the case with the wapiti, so it is very likely that they will outlast the big deer in this open country. It would seem that wolves have a far better chance to run down and capture the young of the wapiti, as the sheep are very much at home among the crags where the wolf must move with very great caution.

I recall stalking a small herd of sheep, which I had followed for ten miles across the rolling uplands, finally locating them in a deep bowl of an exceedingly rugged range of mountains surrounded by high jagged cliffs. As I cautiously approached the sheep from below I encountered a large wolf just about ready to spring upon the sheep from above. The wolf slunk away among the crags, startling the sheep, which broke away toward an outlet far among the cliffs at the upper end of the bowl.

I fired at the ram as it neared the skyline several hundred yards away. The animal went down with a crash on the rim of the bowl. I expected to see it come tumbling down into the deep basin, but just as it was weakening in its struggling and floundering the wolf I had routed from far below rushed out along the rim of the bowl and viciously attacked the prostrate sheep, toppling it over the skyline and out of sight.

It required more than an hour for us to reach the place where the sheep had gone down, only to find that the wolf had rolled and dragged the trophy into a deep chasm, into which we dared not venture on account of the late hour in the afternoon. The wolf seemed to know the only possible exit for the fleeing sheep, and made good in his attempt to reach the point and intercept the animals. I deplored very much losing this fine ram in this way, but there was no help for it.

In all we secured seven specimens of *Ovis camosa,* and then agreed not to shoot another. I would give much today for the head of one of these wonderful rams, but if again given the chance to hunt them, would refuse to shoot one for my own use.

I shall always remember the majestic bearing of certain rams at which I had fair chances had I cared to fire, but which I permitted to look me over and walk away unmolested. I would rather remember them in this way than by a mute head hanging upon my wall testifying to the passing of one of the finest of the big-horn group.

X

Wapiti Hunting

To speak of wapiti among American sportsmen is to talk about something not immediately recognized by many hunters, but to mention elk is to talk in terms understood by all. The facts are, however, that the wonderful animal, *Cervus canadensis*, of our wooded Northwest is not the true elk at all, but is the wapiti, and is in all probability an offshoot from the big stag of Central Asia.

If the theory now advanced by many scientists is true, the wapiti of Central Asia led the nomad of Mongolia across the narrows now known as Bering Straits, the animal to become the American elk and the man to become the American Indian. However true this hypothesis may be, it would seem to be a fact that the so-called elk of the American Northwest is close kin to the giant stag of Asia. The true elk is a large deer with palmated horns common to Scandinavia.

There has been considerable discussion in recent years as to the number of distinct species of wapiti to be found in Asia, and even to-day it is not definitely decided just where to draw the line between the seemingly different species of stag found in Manchuria, Mongolia, and northern China. It has been practically agreed, however, that there are no less than ten species to be found in this area, and I have within the past year definitely located what seems to be an entirely different species in the mountains of Fukien Province in southern China.

111

The wapiti found in northern Shansi Province is a wonderful animal, very closely allied to both the Manchurian
and Kansu species, though possibly being sufficiently
different yet to prove it to be another species of this handsome deer found in Central Asia.

The wapiti by nature is an animal of the heavily wooded
wilds. When it was proposed to me in 1919, after winding
tip a most successful expedition after big-horn sheep (*Ovis
camosa*) in Shansi, that we move along three days' journey
on horseback to the east in order to hunt the great stag,
I took it as a joke, knowing the mountains in that region
would be as equally denuded of all tree life as were those
where we had hunted big horn. But being assured over
and over again by the Mongol guides that we would find
herds of wapiti feeding like cattle on the barren mountains,
it was not difficult to persuade ourselves to remain over
another week or ten days in the far north during the bitter
cold in order to secure a series of this rapidly disappearing deer.

To find the big horn sheep among the barren mountains
was no strange thing, for that animal has every advantage
over the enemies of earlier days, as it is very much at
home on the rugged cliffs and crags where it has been
able to care for itself. The advent of the high-power rifle
in China, however, supplemented by the building of railroad from Peking northward to within a few miles of the
sheep country, seals the doom of both sheep and wapiti.
Three years ago it cost us nineteen days' travel on horseback in order to get specimens of the big horn and the
wapiti, but to-day the same places can be visited by
sportsmen with but very little effort. The finding of these
wonderful animals in northern China will soon be a thing
of the past.

Leaving the sheep country, our route led along the foothills skirting the fertile Kweihuacheng plain. This city is
destined to become the gateway to both the Gobi and

Ordus desert regions, both of which will some day blossom and produce as a garden spot under the skilled hand of the Chinese farmer.

The Mongol is a nomad by nature, spending his time in the saddle hunting and rounding up herds. These vast arid regions will always remain desert unless cultivated by the Chinese, who are gradually filtering into the country, converting the barren grasslands into wonderfully productive fields and gardens.

By making forced marches we could have reached the wapiti country in two days, but an accident, which landed our cart containing specimens and supplies bottom-side-up across a chasm, delayed us a full half day. It was fortunate that our entire outfit was not dashed to pieces at the bottom of this pit across which the cart rested like a well-placed bridge. The ropes which had been securely laced around the loads held things in place to such an extent that we really lost nothing more than our patience, and the few things carried in open carriers.

This experience is but one of the vicissitudes of travel in such a country. Let it be understood that one pays dearly for every trophy he takes out of this mountainous region, where patience and endurance are assets indispensable to the sportsman.

As we approached the region where the hunters assured us there were both wapiti and roebuck in abundance, Mr. Andrews laughingly said, "Caldwell, I would as soon expect to find a snow-man standing on Fifth Avenue in July as to find either wapiti or roebuck in such open country as is ahead of us."

After establishing ourselves in a small village jammed in a nook under the overhanging cliffs, we prepared for our first wapiti hunt. Leaving camp at an early hour in the morning, we followed the frozen stream-bed through a most wonderful gorge until we emerged into more open uplands. There were still no trees or cover in sight, and we wondered all the more where the big deer would conceal themselves.

Far up at the head of the ravine we had traveled for four hours was a vast grassy plateau, cut deep here and there by ravines into which the sun never shines. Our guides now began to talk in whispers, and to scan the snow-covered slopes with care. We began to see many signs of wapiti, and all was tense as we approached the mouth of a ravine sparsely wooded with low blasted birch.

My companion turned up the wooded ravine while I was led on toward the uplands. Soon there were roebuck scampering around in large numbers from the sparse cover through which the others were working their way. The guides also put up three wapiti out of this cover, which gave me my first glimpse of one of these huge wild deer. The Mongols did not seem the least perturbed at seeing these animals disappear over the skyline. There were two cows and a bull carrying a wide spread of horns. Mr. Andrews saw the big bull behind a gnarled birch at close range, but could not maneuver for a shot on account of the lay of the land.

After climbing out of the head of the ravine that I had followed for more than four hours I crossed a mile of rolling uplands with patches of drifted snow showing signs of deer everywhere. When within six hundred yards of a sparsely wooded slope across a shallow ravine I saw a dark object looking much like an upturned stump standing out against the snow.

Raising my glasses I saw a wonderful sight. There stood an immense stag, knee deep in drifted snow, as if guarding eight cows resting in the snow at points but a few yards distant. The bull had a wonderful spread of horns, so I paid no attention to any of the other animals.

Approaching another sixty yards to a point where the slope broke off into the ravine I decided to risk a shot. The bull now gave a sneezing snort and dashed up the hill followed by a mad rush of cows. I fired point blank at the animal as it topped the skyline, striking it in the shoulder. It went down in a mass with a thud, but was soon struggling to get over the divide, across which the cows had already disappeared. I fired a second shot through the fleshy part of the neck which did no damage.

The big bull got to his feet and shambled down a slope a ways, where he stood for a time while being bombarded by Mr. Andrews from a long distance, finally going down in his tracks after being hit several times through the body. My first shot had completely shattered the left shoulder, part of the ball ripping great holes through the lungs, while the metal jacket passed through the right shoulder blade and was found just under the skin on the off side. It was a demonstration of the terrific shocking power of the 250-3000 cartridge.

It is quite a task to skin out an animal of this size on the bleak barrens of the far north with the strong wind from the deserts sweeping across the uplands. After the job was finished we started one of the hunters to camp with the skin and head while we continued our hunt.

A few days later my companion routed a large cow and yearling calf from some cover where he had put up and fired at a roebuck. I crouched low, letting these animals pass me at less than thirty yards distance. I was soon rewarded, for I could see far up the glade the horns of a big bull glistening in the sunlight as he raced down toward me. He doubtless had caught some sign from the cow as she passed me indicating danger, for instead of following her he swung far to the right, coming into sight far up the creek-bed I had been following. At the crack of the gun the animal collapsed in the stream. I saw that he was unable to proceed farther, so watched him slowly get on his feet and walk away from me with an unsteady gait.

I knew the animal was shot through the lungs, so waited to see how long it could remain upon its feet. After slowly walking up the stream bed thirty yards it stood for a few seconds and then toppled over at the foot of an abandoned terrace. This too was a very fine specimen, though not as large as the first one taken.

There is a combination of forces militating very decidedly against the wapiti in this open country of northern China. In the first place, there is absolutely no cover in the region other than dwarfed wild pear and blasted birch. This scant cover is fast being destroyed by fuel gatherers who daily make excursions with donkey trains after wood, which they market at fabulous prices in the settlements on the plain. Thus the big deer is constantly exposed to dangers either while at rest in such cover as can be found, or while feeding on the grassy slopes.

The second factor auguring evil for this splendid animal is the fact that the horns while in the felt are very valuable for medicinal purposes, bringing as much as three hundred dollars a pair in the city markets. For this reason wapiti are rounded up and much persecuted annually.

I very much wanted to get another goral, so we decided to take a day off from hunting wapiti and go up among the cliffs after these fine little goats. It is easy to locate them but exceedingly difficult to get a shot except at long range.

My guide frantically beckoned me to come to him. He was looking off toward a point of the cliff fully a half mile away, and far above us. I could see nothing with the naked eye, and only two faint spots by use of my field glasses, which I could not discern to be living objects. The man declared that these were goral, but if so, it seemed to me impossible to get a shot. After some consultation he intimated to me that we would work our way up to the base of the cliff, while the other man made a wide detour in order to get on top of the range. It seemed a big program, involving hours of time with but little hope of getting a shot, but these men know pretty well what they are doing.

My climb across a ravine and up the slope to the position the hunter had indicated stands out as the most strenuous work that I did on the whole expedition. Soon after we had reached our positions I saw the head of the other hunter appear far up on the top of the precipice. My man signaled him to make the drive.

To me it seemed that there was absolutely no chance for any animal to get down the face of the cliff to where we were. As we waited my guide said, "Be ready when the goat comes, for it will come very quickly."

I sat with rifle in a position for a quick shot. Suddenly a gray object shot zigzaging back and forth from point to point on the face of the cliff, followed by a second. I would not have believed it possible for any animal to come down that precipice as did those two gorals had I not seen it. They both disappeared from view for an instant, to appear again not one hundred feet from us, and then only as they lunged from one high point to another point fifty feet below.

I raised my rifle and fired when the first animal was midway between the two points. It turned over just enough to land upon its back on the point with force which wedged it in between two rocks. The second animal landed squarely upon the first. There was no other place to land, and one was following the other so closely that there was no time to change its course. The second animal made another flying leap into what looked like open space to me and disappeared.

I found that I had struck the animal at which I had fired in mid-air behind the shoulder, totally obliterating the heart. It was by far the most wonderful, though likely largely accidental, shot I ever made with a rifle. It is the kind of a chance that the sportsman often has to take, however, when out after these wonderful little cliff goats.

Our last day after wapiti added another fine bull to our series. We had routed a herd from a draw, being driven

from above when my companion fired at a roebuck which
ran temptingly close. The big deer broke back up the hill
almost running over the eight beaters. The rest of the
day was spent wandering from one patch of possible cover
to another trying to locate the herd. They had scattered,
as we only found two of them at widely different places. I
had a wonderful opportunity to watch one fine bull making
his getaway from the beaters. It was a most satisfactory
study, though the animal was just a little too far for a
shot, and since it was so nearly a duplicate of the second
one that I had shot I really cared little about securing it.

I had been using on this trip peep sights kindly loaned
me by my friend Castle, with whom I hunted serow in
Chekiang Province. But this morning I had replaced them
with my own open sights, hoping to find an opportunity
for trying them out at long range in the wonderfully clear
atmosphere of the far north. We had long since headed home,
and Andrews had his rifle thrown across his shoulder with
a sling. We were traveling down a deep ravine single file
when I heard a rustling in the brush far up to our left.
Looking up I saw a big wapiti bull just breaking cover. I
took quick aim and fired, splintering a sapling just over
the back of the deer, bringing it to a sudden halt. My
second shot, which was fired before my companion could
get his gun in shape for action, grazed the back of the
animal.

It was impossible for me to line my sights in the darkness of the deep ravine, so that I was shooting with very
coarse bead and consequently shooting high. Mr. Andrews
by this time was ready for a shot, and, falling upon one
knee, he took careful aim through his peep sights and
brought the giant stag rolling down the slope. It was a
beautiful specimen, but smaller than either of the other
specimens taken. With a series showing a varied spread
of horns we were satisfied with our hunt, agreeing not to
take the life of another one of these wonderful animals.

These were wonderful specimens, representing the most magnificent species of living deer, yet I saw fossil heads taken from the valley of the Feng Ho which showed a much larger horn than any of the deer taken by us. The same was true of the fossil big-horn sheep taken in the same region. These with other fossils recently collected serve to show what wonderful fauna once inhabited that area at the time when it was most probably heavily forested. The living specimen of to-day, though magnificent, do not compare in size with the fossil dead representing the fauna of a few thousand years ago.

XI

Southern China Wild Boar

Unfortunately for those who would make a careful comparison of the wild hogs of different parts of Central Asia, there are but meager data upon which to work. The study has gone just far enough to determine the fact that there are several distinct species of boar found in China, without establishing records for any group. While the China wild hog may compare in size with that of India, the tusk measurements of the latter are very much larger than anything ever recorded from China. So far as I have read nothing to exceed a ten-inch tusk has been definitely reported from the China species, while boar have been taken in India with a tusk measurement nearly fifteen inches in length. But again it must be remembered that nothing has been recorded from China which can be considered a maximum size.

Shansi province, in the north, offers very fine wild-hog shooting, where the animal is found during the fall and early winter feeding in the forests of dwarf oak. As elsewhere, in this province herds of hogs do a great deal of damage to crops, thus becoming a nuisance to the farmers, who are always happy to have hunting parties come in and scatter the herds, driving them back into the hills.

Hog-shooting is also quite a sport in central China, where it is generally accompanied by an organized drive. It is commonly reported by sportsmen that the meat of both the above species has a tendency to be rather strong in the old hogs. This is not true with the Fukien hogs, for the largest boar killed by me have been both tender and delicately flavored. Wild-hog meat is pronounced almost universally by those who have tried the fresh meat of the young animal most delicately flavored and desirable of all wild game.

Wild-hog hunting offers one of the most attractive sports of all so-called big-game shooting. In Fukien Province almost any shooting worth while is attended by conditions which make a fellow feel he really pays well for the trophies that he gets, but wild-boar shooting is an undertaking calling into play all the patience, strategy, and endurance of the real sportsman.

Personally, I do not term the oft-resorted-to "drive," where the hunter, attended by a gun-bearer, takes his stand upon some divide or runway while a miniature army of coolies armed with horns, gongs and Standard-Oil tins go in to run the game out of the bush, real hunting. There is certainly nothing which savors of the real sport of boar-hunting in this, though it often proves a very effective way of securing a trophy where conditions do not favor a real hunt. Some people are inclined to lose absolutely all that there is worth while in the sport by being prompted too much by the motive of getting a shot, and consequently feel the whole thing has been a failure if game is not driven into the open where an ambush is possible. In this chapter I am not dealing very much with this type of hog-hunting.

In this day of automobiles and automatic guns one gets tired of the pictures so common in the sporting world of cars decorated with game of all kinds, the limit allowed by law always being emphasized. To me this should be discouraged by every person possessing a true sporting spirit.

Game is being rapidly reduced to the point of extinction in parts of China, much to the discredit of the pot hunter.

Not so in Fukien. The game hog would soon starve to death after leaving the plains and foothills where certain kinds of game abound. One must get back into the mountains if real sport is to be had. He who visits Fukien and tramps over the fringe of foothills after pheasant or muntjac in spring or early summer in what the eminent scientist, Edmond Heller, termed a "perfectly atrocious" climate, would little dream of the abundance of game to be found in this same open country during the real hunting season.

The only really easy hunting to be found in the province is in this comparatively open region and on the plains after the great game reservoirs of the north have been broken up by the cold and ice and the stream of life has flowed southward for a few weeks. Geese and ducks with myriads of shore birds and waterfowl pile up on the mud flats and lowlands along the coast.

A visit to one of the larger islands, like the Haitang group, to the south of Foochow, would reveal all this and much more. The appearance of the southbound horde of waterfowl is so sudden and abundant it is as though they had suddenly encountered one of those perpendicular air currents the aviator calls a "bank" and had all "side-slipped" to earth.

Shooting geese and duck during the winter, as can be done along the coast, soon ceases to be a sport to any but the game hog, who is out merely for all he can get. I am almost ashamed to confess that I was party with another man to killing twenty-three wild geese with three shots, and would not dare mention the fact if I could not follow it with the statement that I gave all but one of the birds to natives who were doubly benefited by thus getting some much needed food, and by having their wheat fields saved. The winter wheat and bean crop, and, in fact, all green stuff suffer greatly on account of the inland raids by myriads of the bean goose.

The sportsman who is looking for lots of game and easy shooting had better devote his time to winter hunting along the coast, for wild-hog hunting among the mountains would have no attraction for him.

Small herds of wild hogs are to be found in the mountains and hills not far from the large coast cities, but it is not until one gets well back into the mountains proper that one will find such an abundance of hogs as literally to leave signs almost everywhere. But be it remembered that signs are always much easier to find than the animal which made them.

The damage sustained by the farmers at the hands of the wild hogs is enormous, it becoming necessary to abandon totally all effort to cultivate vast areas which in former years produced great quantities of rice. Numerous hamlets have been abandoned on account of the annual raids of herds of hogs, which utterly destroyed all the crops. These abandoned homesteads, now overgrown with grass and tangle, offer the most attractive lair for all kinds of wild animals, including the big cat of the jungle.

The largest boars are generally found alone upon the highest mountain plateaus, except during the rutting season, when they may be found with the herd. I was one day crossing a very high rolling plateau in company with a young man who had accompanied me on a bear hunt. We had found no bear, though we did find what our hunter guide insisted for a time was a large bear, so we had a few minutes of real excitement. I too was fooled for several minutes, until I saw the tail of the animal, which, of course, immediately put it out of the bear category altogether. The animal finally proved to be one of the large hog-nosed badgers common to this particular plateau country. It was standing upon its haunches on the top of a huge bowlder rocking back and forth in the sun with hair much ruffled up. In size, shape, and action the animal appeared to be a true bear. It was a very interesting study to watch this animal go through its antics while basking in the sun.

Crossing a mile or so of the rolling table land, we came over a little divide overlooking a small stretch of marsh land grown rank with tall grass and weeds. My young companion looked far across the swale and saw an animal standing half way up the slope on the opposite side, calling my attention to it. I first thought it a water buffalo, common to the country and to just such a place, but soon realized that it was a rather out-of-the-way place for any domestic animal, so took a second look to see that the animal was a huge wild boar.

I was using my favorite gun, the 250-3000 Savage rifle. The hog lunged forward and started as only a boar can diagonally across the slope. I fired hurriedly, turning it a little into a straightaway, except for the zig-zagging movement of the animal which rendered an accurate aim exceedingly difficult. I followed the target in the irregular motion until my ivory bead showed plainly between the shoulders, when I pressed the trigger. The boar lunged high in the air, striking the ground dead.

My companion turned upon me and, after looking me over in a rather queer way, said, "Why, you did kill it, didn't you?" He was not a great deal more surprised over the shot than I was myself. I found my first shot had inflicted a flesh wound on the left ham, which accounted for the irregular motion of the animal, rendering the second shot so difficult.

I am convinced, that with the exception of the serow, there is no big game in southern China more difficult to get a shot at than is the wild hog. While I look upon driving as the least sportsmanlike and interesting method of hunting hogs, still I have on a number of occasions been party to drives, and I have witnessed some most wonderful strategy on the part of a wise old boar when it seemed to have been safely entrapped in what might be termed a closely drawn human net.

I recall one such drive when a boar of unusual size was thus rounded up and driven over a comparatively open divide in order to give an eminent naturalist visiting me a shot. As the drive proceeded the hog was routed up so as to pass right over this divide. The grass was neither dense nor high on this pass, and we all felt that the scientist would get a shot as the hog headed straight for the pass. I followed the trail of the pig into the open territory of the pass, only to be signaled by the naturalist that he was guarding the animal which was hiding in the open area of the divide.

Accompanying my guest to the spot where he had seen the hog stop, and where he felt absolutely sure it was hiding, we found the tracks showing plainly the method of retreat. The animal had entered the open heading for the pass, but after getting to within three rods of the waiting sportsman had scented or seen him, recoiled and gone through one of those stunts the native hunters have often been led into believing is actually changing into a spirit. Wild hog-hunting is attended with just such uncertainties as these which fill it with thrills.

On another occasion, and near this same spot, I stationed a friend upon a divide after having definitely located a huge boar by walking to within five yards of it while feeding. Upon leaving this man I said to him, "You be on your guard every instant, for I certainly will put the porker over this divide."

Within fifteen minutes we had the hog on the move, directing him toward the divide. My friend was standing between two large pine trees with rifle in hand. I stood off more than one hundred yards where I could plainly see the fun, only to see the big boar follow a smaller one across the divide and within three yards of the pine trees. Supposing my friend had for some reason moved to another position I hurried forward to find him faithfully keeping guard between the pines. He was surprised beyond measure when

I told him that I had seen the hogs pass within a few yards of him, in proof of which I showed him the two fresh tracks on the opposite side of the tree against which he was standing. Thus again it may be seen how these large animals move through the tangle without making enough noise to attract the attention of a hunter in waiting but a few yards away.

One must be prepared to encounter wild hog in the most unexpected place when working in a neighborhood where they are to be found. In June, 1920, a missionary friend of mine spent a few weeks on the mountains seven miles from Yenping City. As he walked out one morning armed with his walking stick he encountered a whole herd of hogs. He stood and counted twenty-two animals in this herd, everyone standing head-on intently watching him at not to exceed thirty yards. No animal seemed either alarmed or of a mind to attack.

To offset the action of these hogs I will relate what another fellow missionary told me. He was hurrying along a mountain trail when he almost stumbled over the disemboweled remains of a man. The blood was steaming, showing how recently had been the tragedy. The hog had been disturbed and irritated in some way, whereupon it had charged the intruder, ripping him open with one slash of the tusks.

I came along one afternoon to find a great commotion among wood-gatherers on an almost barren hill. A boar had been disturbed and had charged the first person in sight, inflicting a very severe wound in the thigh. It charged on down the hill, attacking every person along its line of retreat until nineteen persons were laid out more or less seriously injured. The hog was later reported to me several miles beyond, still running at full speed and covered with froth and foam. It is an exceedingly hazardous thing to run afoul an ill-tempered wild hog, for there is no telling what it will do.

One of the first instructions laid down for me by experienced boar hunters was to have either hat or coat ready to cast at a hog before a shot was fired at it. It was claimed that if the hog became enraged it would most certainly charge under conditions which might render a second shot more difficult when the only chance of escape would be to throw pith hat or hunting coat in front of the enraged animal and then to hurriedly step aside, for the brute would attack the garment with a vicious jab of the tusks and proceed in a straight course. I have on several occasions been charged by wounded or enraged wild boar, but never resorted to this method of escape. I look upon an enraged tusker in close quarters as fully dangerous as a full-grown tiger.

We have long since learned at my mission station not to go out after pheasant or rabbits with a shotgun without taking along a few shells loaded with buck shot or slugs. On the morning before Christmas, 1921, several of us started off to get enough pheasant for a joint mission dinner. When we wound up the hunt we had pheasant, quail, duck, a hundred pound python and a large wild hog, offering quite a variety from which to choose. Of this lot many of the Chinese people would have chosen the snake on account of its flesh being a supposed sure cure for leprosy and itch.

Time and again while out pheasant-hunting I have walked right up on a bunch of sleeping wild hog. My dogs have been attacked and very severely handled on a number of such occasions, and only a well-directed shot now and again has saved me from being charged. I followed a fair-sized hog into the tangle of an overgrown spruce forest to find myself in the very midst of ten or more large hogs. They heard me approaching, of course, but supposed I was but another hog following the one just entering their circle. The first thing that I knew there was a series of coughs and grunts which showed that I was recognized as not being altogether of their number.

I was now within the family circle, with hogs on all sides of me, and not to exceed five yards from me, everyone bent upon defense. By sheer out-waiting the hogs they lost their nerve and began to rush back and forth all around me, becoming more and more panic stricken. One very large animal flashed in sight but a few feet in front of me offering an opportunity for a snap shot which killed the big brute and started what otherwise might have been a charge into a hasty rout.

An hour spent in an oft-frequented lair reveals much that reflects pretty clearly upon the living habits of the wild hog. One thing which will almost certainly be found is the "house" located in some secluded level spot. This so-called house has given rise to many stories, and a great deal of conjecture among the native hunters, opinion varying so much that it is really a difficult matter to conclude to just what use the large dome-shaped hut is most put.

A newly constructed house will cover a ten-foot space, and will stand four feet or more at the apex. It is constructed of bamboo, small bushes, grass, and ferns gathered by the builder. I personally visited scores of lairs and examined many of these houses before I found one actually in use.

While out early one morning with my twelve-year-old boy we worked ourselves right into the midst of a herd in a dense spruce forest. The animals were coming together after feeding all night in the nearby rice fields, and were working their way into the tangle to spend the day. We too were separated, and hogs were working all around us. Under such circumstances it is an easy matter cautiously to approach to within a few yards of the animals, as any slight breaking of the brush does not disturb them. I once crawled on my hands and knees through high ferns almost to within reaching distance of hogs working in a large herd in a mountain ravine.

On this particular occasion I signaled my son to follow me, and I followed slowly behind several hogs working toward an abandoned terrace. Soon I came upon a well-formed hog hut which showed every sign of being in use. We both stood beside the hut listening for the slightest sound inside, but everything was as still as death. Suddenly something happened to show that the house was occupied. Without warning the whole thing seemed to arise almost in our faces and three large hogs shot out the opposite side. Then the hut settled back to normal again.

A herd of wild hog will put a most formidable defense against either tiger or leopard, the stronger always protecting the weaker. My large hunting dog is very regularly marked, and has time and again frightened defenseless natives into hysterics as he came lunging out of a tangle into the path in front of them. He was once mistaken for a leopard by a herd of seven wild hog when I was hunting silver pheasant in the mountains near Yenping, and I had a rare opportunity to make a study of hogs when on the defensive. The whole herd had charged the dog with a tremendous roar when disturbed from their bed, and I, supposing they would break away as I have always been told they would do, rushed around the opposite side of the hill in order to intercept them. Everything being quiet, I slowly walked up to the top of the hill, my dog falling in behind me. My approach through the dry leaves and ferns was very noisy, and the animals could easily have gotten away down the opposite slope into a deep and wooded ravine, but not so, for they huddled for the defensive.

To my great surprise I found the hogs were moving cautiously forward to attack me. Being armed with only a shotgun I stood still to see whether or not the animals would retreat, as it was a rather serious thing to enrage a herd in a tangle of the kind. After waiting for a few minutes I saw the huge head of one hog break the cover of ferns only a few feet from me, followed by others, seemingly bent upon an attack. They were very vicious, and seemed utterly devoid of fear. After I shot down the nearest hog the others did not break rank, but only retreated backward into the cover.

My dog still scenting the pheasants rushed forward and was charged by two hogs only a few yards from me. I dropped one of these where it stood, whereupon the second one only slowly retreated backward into the tunnel leading from the bed. Such experiences are thrilling enough for the most daring, and afford opportunity for a study of the animals when defending their home.

Possibly the most handsome specimen shot by me was a large boar killed near Yenping in 1922. I had brought down on other occasions hogs as large as this one possibly, but never quite such an old timer. I shot it at long range with my 250-3000 Savage rifle as it crossed a fire-break far up on the side of a mountain, the big animal rolling down the steep slope, landing in the fields almost at our feet.

This boar afforded a wonderful study. It had a shield of cartilage nearly three-quarters of an inch thick covering the shoulders like a blanket and extending to behind the fifth rib. This shield was impenetrable to anything but a ball fired from a high-power rifle. Behind this shield to far back on the flanks were the scars of many battles, many being the deep and unhealed wounds and cuts of the rutting season just passed. One would little think any animal would stand up against an antagonist to the point of receiving so many terrible wounds. Every wound and cut was at almost the same angle, showing plainly that it had been sustained while engaged in combat with another tusker trying to reach the vitals between the ribs but protected by this shield of impenetrable cartilage. After studying this animal it is easy to conceive of many a boar even in the prime of life receiving mortal wounds from a rival while engaged in combat.

The most satisfactory study of wild hog I ever enjoyed was when I undertook to accompany a noted hog trailer as he followed a herd for more than three hours. This man is a prodigy. No well-trained hound can be more depended upon to put up the quarry than he. He guarantees upon forfeit not to lose the trail until he has gotten the animal on the move, and for this reason is very much in demand among hog hunters.

On this occasion we took the trail where the herd had left the fields at daylight and started up the mountain to bed up for the day. We followed them through deep ravines and tangles for an hour and then over an almost perpendicular cliff. It seemed the hogs would never turn in for the day. Little would one believe a sow would trail her half grown pigs over such ground and so far when beautiful cover was to be had on all sides.

The human hound never seemed very much puzzled, though now and again he did almost lose the trail on the face of the cliff when he would get down and blow his breath into what seemed to be tracks, always to arise and start in the right direction. It was a wonderful study to watch the man, and I became so interested in this that I little cared whether or not I got a shot at the hogs.

As we worked our way through the tangle on all fours this human dog slowed down and beckoned me to draw near him cautiously. Pointing to the ground on an almost baked surface he whispered, "Hogs very near." There was nothing I could see, though I had spent much of my time as a boy in the woods and prided myself upon my Indian tracking ability. I now realized that I was following a "hound" entirely out of my class. Sure enough, we came upon the herd not twenty yards from where the man had called the halt.

In hog-hunting it is often the little and unexpected thing which turns the tide one way or the other. One morning I was out after a very large and ill-famed boar. As luck would have it I came upon the hog feeding upon the bark of roots which it was digging up. The breaking of the roots and peeling off of the bark could be heard for fifty yards, so without difficulty I approached to within a few yards of the animal. As I began to maneuver for a shot, a cicada, benumbed with cold, dropped from a tree as I passed, and began to spin around upon its back uttering its weird "trouble" call. No doubt this same hog had heard cicadas call this same way many times when attacked by birds, but in this instance it was different some way, for the animal suddenly turned into a statue, and then uttered several vicious challenges, accompanied by the loud champing of its jaws together. Not having definitely located the nature or position of its danger it turned and rushed to safety into a near-by ravine.

Taken all in all, wild pig-hunting, with the many conditions not encountered in any other big-game hunting, is a real sport. There are always those elements of uncertainty about it which make the person really appreciate every trophy he succeeds in getting in the hill country of southern China.

Plate 9

1. This brute was not so amicable as it now looks, having killed and eaten a man only a few hours before I connected up with him. I shot the animal with a 22-caliber high-power Savage rifle at close range, after the animal had charged me from a long distance. This is a bit of real missionary work I have greatly enjoyed, and incidentally have found most helpful in the preaching of the gospel.

2. These people have assembled in a wild rabble to purchase the flesh of a man-eater killed by me in 1914, it finally becoming necessary to call in soldiers to preserve order until the animal was properly skinned for scientific purposes. My cook realized a considerable sum, while I greatly enjoyed the sport as chief salesman in the center of the group.

Plate 10

1. The deep tear glands make the animal look almost ghost-like when standing in the brush looking right at one. This picture gives a pretty view of the horns of a male.

2. A three-hundred pound female taken five miles from Yenping, Fukien, in 1921. With the exception of the takin there is no animal of China more difficult to shoot.

3. The light color showing on the legs of this specimen is the red markings peculiar to the China form. This probably is as fine a picture of a living serow as was ever taken.

4. My young Mongolian guide was exultant over this sheep, for he beat me over the back shouting. "They do not grow bigger." He was overjoyed at having his picture taken with the sheep where it fell.

Plate 11

1. With the skin and head strapped upon his back, the Young guide led the way across the mountains, following trails wherever possible, but always taking the short-cut for camp.
2. Heads of our three largest rams, the central one covering well the expanse of the double doors of the house we were occupying. The hunters affirmed either of the other two compared favorably with anything previously taken. So far as ever reported the central figure marks the world record for this specie, being 19 3/4 inches basal circumference.
3. A tower of Kweihuacheng, wonderfully strategic on account of its location, and destined to become the junction of railroads which will drain the productive areas of the Gobi and Ordos Desert. Representatives of the B. A. T. and other foreign business concerns are taking more aggressive steps to get a real footing in this important center than are representatives of the Church of Jesus Christ.
4. Goral abound on these almost inaccessible cliffs, where they scurry around above the dizzy heights like rats on a corn bin. My first goral plunged more than five hundred feet into this creek bottom, but was picked up without a break upon the skin.

Plate 12

1. The animal had a wonderful spread of horns. Such a trophy is worth going a long ways after; still we steadfastly refused to take a head for ourselves, drawing the line just as soon as we secured the specimens desired for scientific purposes.
2. The big deer where it fell, giving an idea of the barren slopes which are literally tracked as a barnyard by the animals as they feed in the open.
3. The second Wapiti shot on the Mongolian border.
4. It is always necessary to take along an extra man or so to take specimens back to camp. It is important to carefully guard against any possible rubbing off of hair by the ropes. This we did by the liberal use of dry grass wrapped around the thongs wherever it would rub against the skin.

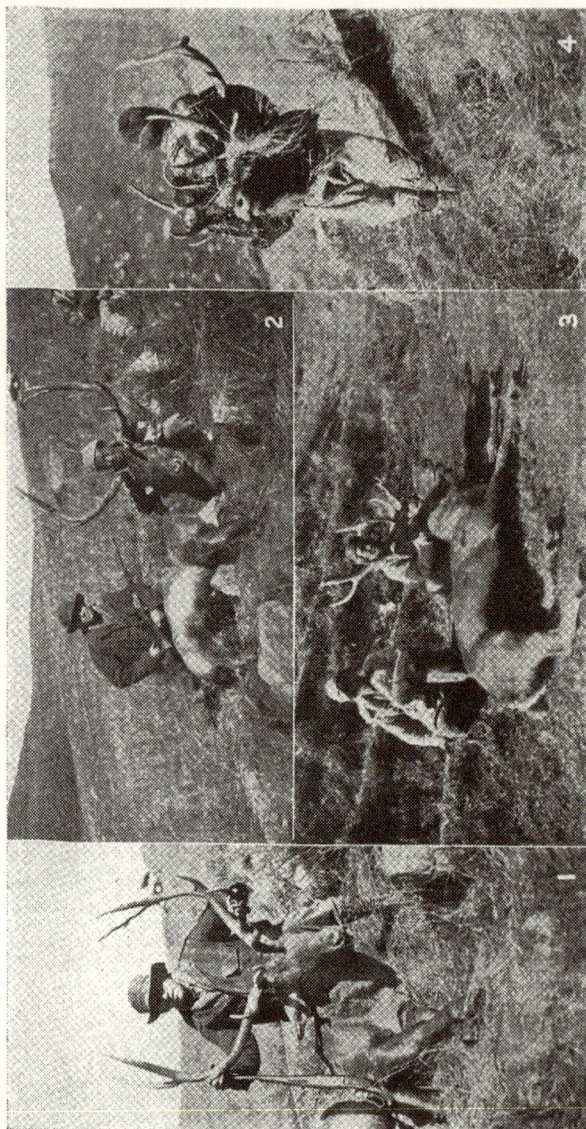

XII

With the Bandits

As long as I am talking about guns and their use, it might be of interest for me to report my observations in another field where arms and ammunition are important, namely, banditry. Much is printed in the newspapers these days about Chinese bandits. But what I write doesn't come from newspapers. I got it first-hand.

My experience with the bandits of northwestern Fukien Province dates back to the year 1916, though brigandage in this immediate region began a few years earlier. The whole period from the beginning of these disturbed conditions until to-day has been characterized by political intrigue and treachery. This is one of the outstanding black marks against the military rule which has been maintained in Fukien ever since the military governor, or tuchün, Li Hau Chi, ousted the civil governor and took into his hands both branches of government. That so-called brigandage ever began, and that it has been perpetuated during these years, reflect great discredit upon the provincial authorities.

In his book, *Camps and Trails in China*, Roy Chapman Andrews outlines in a brief way the origin of brigandage in the Yuki region of Fukien Province. He had visited Yuki City with me and had secured a pretty accurate conception of conditions on that field. At that time I was just getting initiated as "middleman" between the bandits and the military authorities, a most unenviable and thankless job, but one that proved to be a bit of practical service which brought to an end the ruthless and wholesale slaughter of innocent people.

Time and again during the latter part of the year 1921 I was implored by both the bandits and the military to serve again as I had in previous years in this work of reconciliation, but I steadfastly refused. With military generals vying with each other for honors, each ready to resort to intrigue or treachery in order to outdo the other, any man would be a blind fool who would become entangled in affairs of such a serious nature. The most noted bandit chief expressed surprise when I refused to serve the cause of the suffering people as I had once done, and at the same time his representatives assured me that one military general was secretly furnishing him with ammunition with which to fight the others, thus purchasing immunity from raids by the bandits into his territory. At this particular time I was shown a dispatch from this general to the military governor in Foochow in which he boastingly declared that not so much as a bandit track could be found in the whole area over which he ruled. In this way he hoped to discredit the other general and have his own bailiwick enlarged.

It is my purpose in this chapter and the next to relate certain experiences I had while engaged in this work among the bandits. In order to get the exact setting as to who the bandits were, how outlawry on the Yuki field began, and how it was perpetuated, I will briefly recount some of the steps leading up to the terrible conditions that now involve a fair share of the upper end of the province.

Ten or more years ago there was a rather severe famine in the Yuki region. The suffering among all classes of people was acute on account of a sudden shortage of rice. At that time this immediate region was one of the most prosperous in the province, there being a great many families and clans possessing great wealth. But wealth without rice is of little avail in south China. Consequently there was great distress on account of the crop failure of this particular year.

Living in one corner of the Yuki County was a wealthy but generous-minded man named Su Ek. This man had his bins filled with rice from previous harvests, in keeping not only with the ways of the wealthy farmers but of the government as well. There are government bins and store-houses where age-old rice is stored in great quantities against some evil day.

The suffering of the people moved Su Ek, and he took up the matter of disposing of his store of rice on famine rations with other wealthy farmers. It was agreed between these men that Su Ek should first open his bins in order to relieve the suffering, letting the people have rice in limited quantities at a reasonable price agreed upon. The thing went on until one day a throng of people gathered around empty bins at Su Ek's home, but they were assured that by going to another wealthy farmer, living at no great distance across the Dehwa County border, they could get rice on the same basis.

Upon reaching the home of this man the people were met by a rude rebuff. They were told they could have rice all right, but at no such price as Su Ek had been fool enough to sell his for. The price being prohibitive, and all arguing and pleading on the part of the people of no avail, they asked the farmer to stand aside while they helped themselves to a portion of rice each, leaving their money upon the door-sill. This episode brought to an end the rice supply for the famine sufferers.

Things went along as usual, with attending suffering on account of famine conditions. In the meantime this second would-be benefactor disappeared from his home. It was generally believed that he was dodging the criti-cism being heaped upon him on account of his selfish conduct, but instead he was in Foochow making a deal with certain unprincipled military men for an expedition into the Yuki region for "bandits."

All these military officials were thinking about was the using of the dead bodies of so-called bandits as stepping-stones for promotion, so it was no difficult thing to work up great enthusiasm among both officers and privates, since they were definitely assured these "bandits" were unorganized and unarmed. The name of the bandit chief was given, with the exact location of his village and home. This was Su Ek, the benefactor and friend of the people. The names of all the villagers known to this patriotic informer as having participated in the episode at his rice bins were also given, as well as others against whom he had an old score, the more prominent being listed as officers under the noted bandit chief, Su Ek.

Some days later, and without the least warning, bands of soldiers swooped down upon the township, arresting as bandits many innocent people in order that a big bag of brigands might be reported back to Foochow. Su Ek, learning what was going on, succeeded in escaping into the forest behind his home. Soon placards offering a big reward for this man dead or alive were posted throughout the township. This was the beginning of sorrows for that wooded area of upper Fukien Province where conditions favor outlaws.

Taking advantage of the presence of so many soldiers in the neighborhood who were ready to stoop to anything for a dollar, efforts were made to settle all kinds of old scores through secretly accusing persons with whom one wanted to "get even." No man was safe. Blackmail became the order of the day. Naturally, persons with means suffered first. The thing spread rapidly, and, since it had become a source of ready revenue for the soldiers, their numbers increased greatly. Scores of people of weaker clans, fearing they would be secretly informed upon by stronger enemies, went into hiding in the hills.

These helpless people, whose numbers had reached into hundreds, naturally rallied around Su Ek, who was suffering banishment and worse on account of kindness shown them and their families. Many influential people succored those who were hiding in the hills by sending them food and supplies. Such as were informed upon were arrested and executed without trial, while their property was confiscated. Extortion became very common throughout the disturbed area, the well-to-do having to purchase immunity from false charges at exorbitant prices.

Brigandage had thus been forced upon an innocent people, for in order to live at all agents were sent to the coast to get in touch with those who were ready to supply guns and ammunition. What had for six months been a defenseless horde of hounded refugees in the hills suddenly burst forth upon the soldiers quartered in their own homes and desecrating their womanhood. The soldiers were helpless and cowed before the onslaught of these outraged mountaineers who forced them into conflict in order to wreak vengeance. The military has never ceased to rue the day it forced brigandage upon this people.

I once met a noted bandit chief who, at the outbreak of this trouble, was a prominent merchant in a large walled city several days distant from Yuki. In order to settle some clan feud from a previous generation he had been secretly informed upon as a purchasing agent for the bandits. Without warning his place of business was visited by a battalion of soldiers, who arrested him and dragged him off to Yuki, where he was tried before a military court as being a bandit. His father and mother had already been brutally killed by the soldiers, and the ancestral home looted and burned. He too would have been executed had not the elders of eighty villages come forward with a petition for his release, with a signed guarantee that he was an innocent man. He was finally released, whereupon he returned to his business in the distant city.

Being possessed of considerable means, he immediately erected another house upon the ancestral home site.

Not many months elapsed when another force of soldiers came into the Yuki region, and, not being satisfied with the revenge they had already wreaked upon the clan, charges were again preferred against the merchant by the enemies of his ancestors. The merchant took the precaution to be on his guard upon learning that a new force of soldiers had reached his distant township. Sure enough, in the course of a few days a band of soldiers entered the city where he was doing business. Of course they missed their man, who secreted himself in a place of safety. The soldiers returned to Yuki and applied the torch to the new home of the man, and issued notice of a reward for noted bandit So-and-so.

This was enough. The merchant returned to his native township and rallied about him a group of relatives and sympathizers who had been driven to the hills. This was the nucleus of one of the most formidable bands of bandits ever known in the region. Great indeed was the toll in lives this man exacted from the northern soldiers during the next few years. I met him one day by appointment far back in the hills during my work of reconciliation. In order to keep faith and meet me at the time and place agreed upon he fought three battles with the soldiers, losing several men in the engagement, but cutting to pieces three forces of northern troops.

Thus group after group of bandits was formed, first by a mere score or more of helpless people rallying around some leader bent upon revenge. Leaders were always chosen by this process of natural selection. Guns were brought in from the coast, some being accompanied by ammunition, while others were obsolete and useless. Wooden guns were furnished a few of the more daring young men, and with these in hand raids were made upon the richest members of the offending clans.

Men, women, and children from such homes were captured and taken into the hills where huge sums of money
were exacted from them as ransom by the method known
among the brigands as the use of the "wedge." The two
thumbs were placed together, knuckle to knuckle, and
over them was placed a ring made of plaited hemp. A small
wedge was then inserted between the knuckles. This wedge
was gently tapped with a mallet when the bartering began. I
have known of ten thousand dollars thus being extorted
from one individual, but always the deal is accompanied
by much haggling and bartering.

With money thus secured, guns and ammunition were
purchased in quantities from Japanese agents who soon
took advantage of the disturbed conditions. Soon formidable bands of bandits were scattered over the country,
bidding defiance to the soldiers huddling in forts erected
in the villages below.

I was shown four old, obsolete, bolt-action military
rifles which a bandit chief told me had been but a few
days before purchased from a Japanese agent for one
thousand dollars each, and one dollar each for the cartridges. Money now came easy and the bandits were willing
to pay any price for guns and ammunition. With the arming
and organizing of the bandits, the northern soldiers were
up against a proposition that they were utterly unable to
handle. The soldiers from the barren hills of Shantung
were terrified and helpless when forced into battle with
these men of the southern mountains.

Until the bandits became armed they avoided clashes
always. One chief said to me, "We fight only when we want
to, but when things favor us we force the soldiers into
battle whether they want to fight or not."

The organization and discipline of the bandits was a
surprise to every one, but to the military officers who
engaged them in battle most of all. The soldiers soon
learned that the bandits were to be dreaded, and often

rather than go against them in battle a battalion of troops would mutiny, killing its officers and join the bandits. The bandits did not want the men, but did want their guns and ammunition. The latter they kept, but disposed of the former in ways that best suited them.

One band of thirty soldiers killed its officers and joined the bandits, taking many thousands of rounds of ammunition with rifles and one machine gun. This machine gun has been a source of embarrassment to both bandits and soldiers ever since, for the former can't use it and the latter dare not report it missing to the authorities in Foochow. When I last talked about it with a general he seemed much more interested in getting the machine gun into his possession than he did about suppressing brigandage.

Almost always soldiers sent out to disperse the bandits would fire volley after volley into the air upon approaching the village where the bandits were spending the night, or resting as the case might be, and, after the bandits had withdrawn, if they did not care to give battle, the soldiers would swoop down upon the village, pillaging and burning everything before them. The village elders or others would be arrested and executed on the ground that the village had entertained bandits. Whole communities of innocent and helpless people have thus been scattered or blotted out, the heads of the elders often being sent in as evidence of a victory over the bandits, or military prowess.

The thing has also worked in reverse order. The soldiers would take up quarters in a community, occupying always the best homes. During their stay the villagers would have to spread the very best to be had before the soldiers, sacrificing hogs and cows without hope of remuneration. When the soldiers would withdraw the bandits would descend upon the place and apply the torch.

Thus the towns and hamlets in the rural regions found themselves literally between the millstones. Whole communities of hundreds of homes have been absolutely annihilated.

My first trip to interview a bandit chief took me through a township which only a few months previously had consisted of scores of prosperous villages and towns. Absolutely nothing remained even to suggest what had once been except the piles of debris marking the sites of the once happy towns.

On the river bank stood a spreading banyan tree under which one petty military officer executed during one afternoon scores of innocent people, rolling their headless trunks into the river, but saving the heads as trophies to show the higher-ups.

It was into scenes like this that I entered in the spring of 1916 to begin my work of reconciliation. The harrowing tales of suffering and bloodshed were of a character to make me worse than sick at heart, for time and again I have been nauseated by what I have looked upon.

In April of my first year in this region I visited Yuki City, where I was to meet all the district preachers and workers in a conference on evangelism. From every township came stories of the abuses perpetrated by both soldiers and bandits. This was my first contact with that of which I had heard for several years, and I was amazed at the degree of suffering inflicted upon the innocent people under the guise of adjusting the bandit business. It was very evident that even the heartless military authorities outside knew but little of what was actually going on behind the rugged mountains.

I learned of a tragedy which had taken place but a short time before. This is but one of the many deeds of treachery which have been consummated in connection with this bandit business in Fukien, and is related here for no other purpose than to give the reader the real setting of affairs at the time that I threw my hat into the ring.

One high military official conceived the idea of effecting terms with the bandits rather than undertaking to exterminate them, as he had been commissioned by the

authorities in Foochow to do. A few clashes with these
men, who had their outlawed position forced upon them,
was enough to convince this general that it was utterly
useless to try to subjugate them, so he set about in perfectly good faith compromising the affair, granting amnesty
to all bandits who should turn in their guns and ammunition and return to their homes. This was exactly what
the bandits wanted to do, so the affair was easily arranged.
In order to give confidence, one of the Chinese ministers
of the Methodist Episcopal Church was asked to serve as
a middleman.

Everything having been arranged to the satisfaction
of all concerned, the bandits turned in scores of guns
and thousands of rounds of ammunition at the time and
place agreed upon. There was widespread rejoicing over
the way this matter had been disposed of by the general,
while scores of homes were gladdened by the return of an
outlawed father or son. That was one of the happy days
of 20th Township, Yuki.

General Wang proceeded to Foochow to report to
Tuchün Li Hau Chi, under whose orders he was acting.
Sixty miles below Yuki City, and at the head of steam
navigation, he met a special military commissioner by the
name of Ding, who had been asked by the Tuchün to proceed to Yuki to render any assistance possible in adjusting the brigand affair. General Wang reported to him what
had been accomplished, announcing his purpose of proceeding the following morning to Foochow to render a report
to the Tuchün. Commissioner Ding said he would proceed
to Yuki City, there to wait further instructions from
Foochow.

It requires about five days to make the trip up these
rapids and five days is ample time for any self-seeking
military man in China to concoct many schemes. This
man saw in what had taken place under the able hand of
General Wang, not only a chance to discredit the general,

but at the same time to seek promotion. He hurried right through to Twentieth Township, where he got in touch with the village elders, to whom he announced the reason for the presence of himself and his soldiers in the community. A mass meeting was called for the following day at which time he would address the people of the township, but especially the ex-bandits, for whom he had a message of the greatest possible importance.

On the following day the people came together to be the guests of the military commissioner, who had prepared an elaborate feast as a token of good faith. During the after-feast speech the commissioner explained the form of a pardon he held in his hand, assuring each ex-bandit that it was especially important that he possess one of these pardons. Not only so, declared the generous commissioner, for if there were any innocent people who were fearful that they might later be falsely accused of having had to do with the bandit business, they too should avail themselves of the opportunity of securing one of these pardons, which would ever stand as security against any such false accusations.

After the matter was repeatedly explained until everyone present understood perfectly the import of the "pardon" being displayed, the doors of the ancestral hall were thrown open and the people were invited to enter one by one in order to receive their pardon.

As the people in their enthusiasm hurried into the door of the ancestral hall they were halted by soldiers who permitted only one person at a time to enter. It was not until one hundred and sixty men had been trapped in this way that it became known what was going on inside the hall. As the people entered they had been seized by soldiers and bound with cords. After the thing became known and the people scattered, the one hundred and sixty were led out in front of the ancestral hall where they had feasted an hour earlier and were executed.

That they had applied for a pardon was confession that they had been bandits, reasoned the commissioner as those who had acted as middlemen tried to stay the dastardly work. One petty official cut off the heads of thirty men. He slashed off heads until his sword became bent. While straightening it under his foot the Methodist minister who had served as one of the middlemen arrived upon the scene. He hurried forward and rebuked the heartless wretch, who only responded by saying, "With the ease the farmer puts the sickle to standing grain I put my sword to the neck of men."

The remonstrance on the part of the middlemen delayed for a few hours the execution of a few, but saved no man. All of these men, many of whom possibly had never had anything to do with the bandits, were put to death, and the commissioner reported that he, with a little handful of soldiers, had engaged in battle a large force of armed bandits, capturing or killing the entire lot. He reported counting on one battlefield one hundred and sixty dead bandits who had fallen under the stroke of his men. As a reward for this prowess, this man was promoted and is now a general.

The preceding is one instance of the treachery which had characterized the dealings on the part of the representatives of the government prior to my first visit to the Yuki field. On the morning of my second day in Yuki City I was told of the depredations of a large tiger at a village three miles from the city, and was implored by the pastor of the Methodist church in the place to go and dispose of the animal. At the urgent request of the workers present I decided to spend the afternoon trying to kill the beast.

As I hurried along the street toward the west gate I learned that there had been an execution of "bandits" during the forenoon. This interested me but little, as it was reported to be an almost daily occurrence, but when I walked out to the gate of the city and saw the number of weeping women standing by a low wall beside the road I realized that I had walked right upon the ghastly scene. So it proved, for just over the wall in an abandoned rice field not to exceed fifteen yards square were the bodies of eleven victims, two of whom were mere children.

Almost at my feet was the head and what seemed smiling face of an eight-year-old boy, while in the opposite corner was a little trunk which I guessed matched the tiny head. It was the most ghastly sight that I had ever looked upon, and I felt for a moment like fleeing from the terrible scene, but my attention was attracted by low groaning from the center of the field. I soon noticed that a blood-besmeared chest of a man lying in the middle of the field heaved with every groan. To my great surprise I found this man, whose neck had sustained a great gaping wound and whose head seemed all but severed from the body, was not only alive but conscious.

Climbing over the mud wall I approached the suffering man and heard him plead for a sip of tea, and then for some one to kill him. His misery must have been that of the damned, yet no man dare extend a hand to help lest he too suffer the same fate. The soldiers were forcing the poor man to live on and suffer, waiting possibly until some person would offer a few dollars to have him put out of his misery.

I stood by this man who was conscious and listened to the story that he had to tell; how, in order to settle some clan score of long standing, members of the rival clan had secretly informed upon him to the soldiers as having been seen buying straw hats for the bandits. That was all that was necessary in those days, and the man had to pay the price, going the way of thousands of his kind.

I went on after the tiger, but could think of nothing but the terrible thing that I had seen and heard. So horribly did the thing loom up before me that it almost unbalanced me, with the result that the tiger I was hunting crept to within ten feet of me unobserved, and would easily have caught me had it not done the unheard-of-thing of growling viciously when it crouched for the final spring.

After disposing of the tiger I could take no interest in it. I hurried back into the city to find that the soldiers had beheaded the poor man, who had lain all day in the parching sun, as custom will not permit the sun to set upon such a scene where life exists in one victim.

The bodies of the victims had been viscerated, and the liver and heart taken into the city by the soldiers and eaten. This was the custom at that time among the soldiers in order to imbibe the spirit of anyone dying with a brave heart. This same cannibal custom was being practiced by the soldiers of the brigadier general in Yenping City in 1921.

Later, too, I met the reaction the same year as I tried to collect funds for the famine sufferers in the north. Scores of people responded to my appeal for famine relief with these words: "These northerners have fed until fat during these years upon the liver and heart of our people in this province; let them now in the north feed upon their own people who have starved to death." It was a sickening comeback upon the conduct of soldiers of a professed republic, but it suggested a fact too true to admit of any argument.

When I ascended the pulpit that evening I said little about the experience that I had had tiger-hunting, but I did enlarge upon the tragedy beside the road, declaring that if the gospel of Jesus Christ could not put a stop to such butchery of innocent people, I would leave China. It was a bold and daring thing to do, and at the time that I uttered the challenge I did not know how I would even go about attacking the thing. Soon the report of what I had said in public got to the brigands, many of whom were eager to return to their homes in peace. My movements after that were very closely watched by the bandit spies, as I soon found out.

The first trip that I made in the country to spend a night in a chapel I was waited upon by three very scholarly men, whom I little dreamed were bandits. These men suggested that possibly the bandits would be willing to put their whole cause in my hand if I would but act as a middleman in the matter of bringing about reconciliation between them and the government. They casually said in parting, "If you do care to undertake this good work, always remember the treachery of Twentieth Township." Before I left the place another man said, "I have been told that the bandit Chief Dang said he would intrust his all to the hands of an American missionary." The confidence these people later manifested in me during long months of work among them was both childlike and implicit.

It is strange how events dovetail through one's life, things of earlier years fitting into important events of the present. I had on one occasion entertained in my home a prominent gentleman who at that particular time was vice-speaker of the House of Parliament in Peking. My only chance, as I thought, was to get this matter before the president through him. Letters and telegrams passed between us, with the result that in due time I received credentials from the Tuchün of Fukien asking me to go out and settle the bandit business if I could, putting absolute power in my hands. My commission from the bandit chiefs carried both absolute power and a confidence that I never would betray.

I now had full commissions from both sides. The question was as to how I could go about this work without an unfavorable reaction upon the church. Should there be treachery on the part of either side, the church would be the sufferer. On the other hand, if it got out that I was acting with such full authority, there might be an undue knocking at the door of the church. I feared one aspect of the thing about as much as I did the other, so before I did any work whatever I had it published abroad that what I was about to do was not for the sake of the government, nor was it for the sake of the bandits, nor was it for the sake of the church, but that it was solely for the suffering people of the disturbed area.

Following this declaration I practically closed the doors of the church for a period of time, making it next to impossible for any person to enroll his name upon the church records. No reformed bandit was to have his name enrolled under any condition for a period of a full year at least. It was a gratifying result of this stand that during the period of my work among the bandits neither membership nor contributions increased, for it soon became understood that the church was in no way involved in what was going on. To make nay position doubly sure, I refused to permit either bandit chief or military officer to defray my traveling expenses. Everything possible was done to safeguard the good name of the church. I soon had communications on the way to four bandit chiefs asking for an interview. Three interviews were immediately accepted, and I began my work among the outlaws the following week.

XIII

Some Bandit Chiefs I Have Known

The way was now definitely open for me to interview several bandit chiefs. I knew absolutely nothing of the geography of the country where these men had retreated into their strongholds: nor did I know anything about the character of the men I was going out to meet other than their reputation for daring deeds. It seemed wise to call first upon Chief Ling Cu Lung, who was notorious for his daring attacks upon the northern soldiers, but whose implicit confidence, for some reason then unknown to me, in the missionary, afforded a promising point of contact in the work ahead.

This man selected as a meeting place a small village hanging on the almost perpendicular face of a chasm where a great notch had been cut through the high range of mountains which stood out with the symmetry of a green wall against the sky. There was absolutely no approach other than by one winding path up a rugged slope, and then along the top of the range for miles, where the road was plainly visible from almost any strategic point across, the chasm. When the road reached a point about two miles from the lonely little hamlet it suddenly dropped abruptly into the chasm and across the wild stream which had bitten this chunk out of the range.

The road leading from the top of the range into the chasm was in such plain view from the village on the opposite side as to render possible the distinguishing and counting of figures without the use of glasses. The strategy of this place was very evident to me just as soon as our guide pointed out the village from the distant mountain top, and I realized that these men were taking absolutely no chances when they agreed to meet me at this trysting place.

I had with me a high military officer and a special deputy from the Tuchün in Foochow, in addition to my own interpreter, cook, and burden-bearer. I could, of course, converse directly with the bandits, but on account of the presence of these military men from the north who could not understand a word of the language of the Fukien people, it was necessary to take along a man who could be ears for them to know all that I was saying. I insisted upon this. I had been instructed by the bandits not to bring along any extra men, so I had previously sent in a list of those who would accompany me. It was pointed out to me that there was great danger of being fired upon if I took along a greater number than I had designated.

I learned later that these bandits had been informed by agents of those parties who were getting rich supplying arms and ammunition that I was to take a lot of soldiers under the guise of servants and coolies, and that during the night these people would arise and attack the bandits. I soon realized the situation I faced in seeking interviews with these brigands, but I have never had any dealings with a more straightforward lot of men than these same outlaws.

I had no asset worthwhile among these people other than that I was a missionary, and an American, but I resolved in the very beginning that I would permit nothing that would impair the confidence that these men were manifesting. I refrained from being so much as seen in conversation with any of my own party except under conditions wholly above suspicion.

Upon reaching the village overhanging the tumbling stream, looking now like a silver thread resting upon the tops of the laurel and rhododendron in the depths of the canyon, I was led into a beautifully decorated room where a feast was spread. Everything was normal in the village and there was no one in sight whom I could so much as suspect of being a bandit. One distinguished-looking man came forward and talked with us for a time, until evidently he became satisfied that everything was all right, whereupon he announced to me that the, brigands had not yet arrived, but that he had been asked to prepare a supper for us. He then said that the bandits would not arrive from a far distant point until nine o'clock in the evening, but that we were to make ourselves at home in the village. At that time sharp-shooters were watching us from close by.

Though weary from my twenty-mile tramp over the rugged mountains I greatly enjoyed the following two hours studying the making of paper from bamboo pulp. The interest I manifested in this industry and in things in general seemed to gain for me the confidence of all the villagers. Young men began to slide down through the bamboo groves back of the village as if in response to some signal. We talked of paper-making, of wild boar-hunting, and of everything that I thought would interest these people. Finally, I began to talk of education, to find that there never had been a school in the community. Yet there were a number of young men who could read well, and talk intelligently concerning many problems of the outside world.

It developed that these young men as boys had studied in Christian day schools in distant townships, and it was their knowledge of the church and of the missionary that was responsible for the attitude of confidence on the part of the chief toward me. They themselves were bandits of the most daring type. They were the very brain of the gang of outlaws, and it required much real brain work to exist at all in the kind of life these people were forced to live.

During this first night with the bandits I learned the true character of the men with whom I was dealing. Only a few days after my visit, and before the last details of the matter were definitely fixed up, one of the very men who sat with me almost all night around the council table was stood against a tree and shot by his fellows because he had acted in a way that brought discredit upon the gang.

Upon being summoned to supper we were ushered again into the room where the ruby light from the many lanterns made a wonderfully beautiful glow. I found a table spread with such a sumptuous feed as one would little expect to find in such an out-of-the-way place. The chopsticks were of carved ivory, and many of the dishes and utensils of rolled silver. I had never seen anything like it in the homes of the rich, and must have manifested my surprise at the elaborate occasion.

As we were being seated around the table with the usual haggling and commotion common to such doings, a man whispered into my ear, "The chief has done you a great honor in preparing such a spread." I realized this forcibly enough, but felt a keen disappointment because no person whom I could imagine as being a bandit was being seated with us at the table, for I had hoped to meet these men in sufficient numbers to permit a study of them.

I found a little later, however, that they were near at hand in numbers sufficient to satisfy anyone. This was my first appearance among the bandits, and Chief Ling

had been cautioned by all the other chiefs to play absolutely safe lest another trap be sprung by the military.
The eyes of at least four bands of bandits were watching
what was going on in the isolated little hamlet, and there
were armed men enough within gunshot to have cleaned
up all the northern soldiers in the province.

Everything went off beautifully during the feast, which
was ordered according to the ways and usages in such
events. I was profoundly impressed with the etiquette of
the occasion, but nearly collapsed when an expression of
confidence of which I had often heard but never seen was
pulled off. I think that it was about the twelfth course
when a large rooster, fairly swimming in delicious gravy
and covered with mushrooms, was brought in. The comb
stood up over the bird almost as broad as one's hand. As
the platter containing the fowl was placed in the center
of the table, and before any move had been made to dis-
member it, the man acting as host in the absence of his
chief arose, and with very great deliberation removed the
comb from the head. With an unused pair of carved chopsticks he placed the comb on a silver tray. Taking the
tray in both hands he walked once around the table with
the air of a priest about to do sacrifice before the gods.
Stopping on his second round at my left, he made a low
bow and with great dignity placed the tray before me.
Realizing the seriousness of the occasion I arose and made
a low bow in recognition of the honor, not understanding
at the time the full meaning of the procedure. The man
sitting to my right leaned over and whispered in my ear:
"You are crowned. This is the greatest token of confidence
known among these people."

The ice seemed now to be broken with a vengeance,
for the several villagers seated about the table, who up to
this time had been silent to such a degree that I was almost

embarrassed at their seeming sullenness, opened up and began to discuss freely with me the whole bandit situation. They appeared to ignore totally the presence of the military men sitting at the table as they lay bare the facts.

Seated at the table were the private secretary of the bandit chief, and others high in authority, who no longer tried to conceal their identity. They had committed into my hands their very lives with this "crowning" ceremony, and I realized as never before what it meant to represent men of this character in a cause of this kind. For a few seconds I almost wished that I was out of the whole thing, but upon more sober reflection I realized that the undertaking was a sure success so far as the bandit side of it was concerned. My task was to safeguard the interests of these sturdy mountain men who had committed themselves without reserve into my hands.

I well knew that if I did not act wisely from the beginning, there might be serious consequences. My first move would have to be made with very great care. What I did staggered the military men who had accompanied me, but it settled once and for all the character of the deliberations. I was assured by the interpreter as we settled down for a few minutes rest just before dawn that I had absolutely sealed the thing and that there would be no attempt at trickery on the part of the military men or those whom they represented. It was a little thing, but the right thing in the right place.

At the very beginning, after the feast table had been cleared, and ten bandit officers who had come in from the hills accompanying their chief had seated themselves, I made known my purpose in asking for the interview, suggesting my relations to the whole matter. I pointed out that the Tuchün, or military governor, in Foochow, had a representative in Mr. Chang; that the commander of the troops assigned to the task of disposing of the bandit matter had a spokesman in the presence of General Wang, enlarging upon the fact that these men acted with the authority of those whom they represented. I then agreed openly to become the representative of the bandits, responsible to them for all that I did or agreed upon. I insisted that my position as spokesman for the outlaws be understood by the other men present in order that there should be no misunderstanding when I stood firmly for fair play, as I assured all present I most certainly would do.

We had been seated around the table an hour or more deliberating concerning the terms for a settlement as they were laid down one by one by either side, when suddenly every bandit at the table jumped to his feet at the whimpering call of an owl from the distance. They jammed about the door manifestly very much excited.

At first I did not realize what had caused the sudden commotion, but sat calmly at my place at the head of the center table. From this position I could look out of the door and far across the deep chasm to the trail along which we had traveled in the afternoon. On this road, and fully three miles away, were a number of moving lights. What they were I have never learned, but the quick eye of some bandit sentinel had seen them at their first glimmer in response to which there floated across the stillness the lonely call of a night bird. This call had electrified the bandits, and every man was soon ready for either fight or flight. It all cast light upon the terrible tension of the hour.

Without moving from my seat, and without showing the least apparent concern, I said, "Brothers, I have agreed to represent you in a faithful way in this important affair, and I mean to do it if you give me the opportunity; I am wholly responsible for what takes place. I bid you be at peace and return to your seats that we may continue the deliberations."

In response to these words each bandit resumed his seat, bowing low and smiling sardonically. One man then resumed his station at the door and watched the movements of the lights. I was just as much interested in the lights as any man present, for not only the success of the task to which I had set my hand, but my own life as well was in the balance. I dared not show the least concern, however, lest there be a stampede into the hills of the men that I had gotten together. I did not get away from the thought of those lights all night, for there was no telling what some aspiring military official might try to accomplish since so many had recently been promoted upon reporting to Foochow some deed of daring against the bandits. I was much relieved when I could see the waving bamboos in the gray dawn, and there was excuse for us to be up and moving about.

My first night in a bandit stronghold was past, and the suspense was over. The deliberations had been entirely successful, as arrangements had been made for the turning in of guns and ammunition, and the time and place for the issuing of pardons agreed upon. Of course the military men were greatly elated, for they could report back to their chiefs the success of the interview, pointing out the degree of success attending *their* efforts, and consequently would expect promotion or reward.

The bandits crowded around me like enthusiastic schoolboys, thanking me for the great service I had rendered them, each eager to know when he could safely return to his home. As bandits these fellows had proven a terror to their enemy. They had exacted heavy toll from the soldiery in every conflict and were now well armed and equipped for better defense than they had ever been able to put up before, but all were eager to quit the business and return to the homes of their fathers. This was the hour of supreme happiness for these several hundred outlaws who had conducted themselves as highwaymen for years, but not as a matter of choice.

Upon leaving the following morning, after a breakfast but little short of the feast of the evening before, the mountains and ravines reechoed the banging of firecrackers and firing of small field pieces. I heard one man say to another, "Our cause is perfectly safe in the hands of that missionary, for he is an American," and I resolved again that it was then, and always should be.

Within a few days all the conditions agreed upon were met and this band of outlaws passed out of existence. Word was passed to the other bandit chiefs and within a short time I found myself overwhelmed in this work of reconciliation.

My next experience found me involved in complications of a very serious nature, from which I had difficulty in extracting myself. I will never forget the night spent with bandit chief Dang Gi Ling. I was strongly advised at the outset not to undertake this trip, but being bent upon rushing the thing through as fast as possible, I was as willing to meet the chief now in his distant stronghold as later at some more accessible point.

I traveled far across the mountains the first day to where I was to spend the night, expecting to proceed the following day to some distant point where. I would meet in person this man of whom I had heard so much. Common rumor had it that I was to be waylaid and assassinated at the instigation of those who were carrying on a lucrative business in guns and ammunition. What I heard only stimulated in me a greater desire to see this bandit, the most dreaded among those operating in this particular region. To put this band out of business would mean the end of more than one form of lawlessness and evil.

The first thirty miles was along a narrow wooded way following for the most part a river basin, and then across a steep divide. From the crest of the divide I could look down into a quiet nest of villages on a wide plain comprising a township. The exact hour of our arrival at this point must have been announced well ahead, though by whom I do not know, as I did not know myself where we were going or when we would arrive. There was a full mile of men, women, and children lining either side of the road, armed with drums, gongs, horns, and oil tins to meet us. This was the second reception I had been extended during the day, but this one was of a character quite different from the one at ten o'clock in the morning.

I was then traveling along the Yuki River far inland. On all sides were the smoldered ruins of towns and hamlets, showing the work of the northern soldier. A terrible struggle had been going on for weeks in this region and it was now a devastated waste. As I rounded a point of land close to the river I saw five boats heavily loaded with armed men running a steep rapid. There was evident excitement in the boats as I was discovered, and one by one they swung into a cove at the foot of the rapid where the soldiers scrambled out to the shore and were soon lost in the heavy underbrush.

Of course I did not know what this meant, but I did recall the warning which had been given me not to start on this particular trip. I did not slacken my pace, however. Walking over a little knoll I came suddenly upon more than one hundred fully-armed men lined up on either side of the narrow trail. This proved to be a military escort sent down the rapids to accompany me through a danger zone within their lines. This soldier-guard convinced me that possibly there was danger lurking along the highway.

After crossing the river miles above I left the soldiers and struck off into the mountains, emerging into the township across the distant divide to receive the second welcome. I was now traveling in territory recognized as being for the time under the jurisdiction of the bandits. There were no armed men to welcome me this time. For the most part they were people who had suffered terribly during these years of disorder. Now they were out of the fullness of their hearts expressing joy at the thought of possible peace and quiet.

I unlimbered my camera to get a picture of the crowd, but everything was so enveloped in a cloud of smoke from the firecrackers that picture-taking was impossible. For nearly half an hour I passed through a double line of people shouting and singing and making more than merry, the lines falling in behind to lengthen my train as we passed. This welcome was not staged by either the bandit chief or the military, but was a spontaneous outburst of happiness and enthusiasm among the hundreds of families who had suffered terribly at the hands of both.

After getting settled down in the room that I was to occupy for the night I was waited upon by three distinguished-looking men who engaged me in conversation. When everyone else was out of the room these men leaned over and asked in a whisper, "Where are the guns?"

I supposed the man was inquiring concerning my so-called "Tiger Gun" which I had been accustomed to carry with me, and which had quite a reputation. I therefore told him that I had left my guns in Yuki City.

"I mean the sixty guns you were to bring to-day to be delivered to Chief Dang," replied the man.

Not knowing anything about the matter, it was difficult for me to evade the issue without creating suspicion. So I simply replied, "Oh, yes, those guns. I will discuss the matter with Mr. Dang tomorrow when I see him," and tried to dismiss it in that way.

These men would not remain long enough even to drink a cup of tea, but hurriedly arose, saying that they would have to hurry back and report the matter to Mr. Dang.

As they were going out I said with a reassuring smile upon my face, "Tell the chief not to worry about the guns; that matter is all right."

They left me satisfied that everything was as it should be, although they were evidently disappointed that the guns had not been delivered.

Just as soon as my visitors were gone I called in the interpreter and laid the matter before him. He knew nothing about any guns being promised. I next called the deputy representing the Tuchün, for I now felt sure that there was some underhanded work being done, and he was the first man that I would suspect of treachery.

To my great surprise, I found that this man had personally taken a representative from the Mayor of Yuki City and one from General Wang and had gone in privately in my name and had interviewed the bandit chief, offering him a high commission in the army, and a second job paying him a big salary, in token of which he was to have sixty of the latest style military rifles and sixty thousand cartridges. This move was carried out on the part of these men simply in order that they might be able to report to their superiors having brought this bandit to terms prior to my getting on the ground, and thus get the glory.

When dealing with ambitious men of this kind one must be ready to meet some such deal at any turn. I was, in fact, expecting to do anything reasonable and was prepared for it, but to confront such a serious proposition as this worried me. However, I was too far along to back out even for a day of consideration and council.

I could but give vent to my wrath, telling the three men involved in the scheme exactly what I thought of them and their way of doing business, but in doing this I had to use great care and talk but little above a whisper. To express wrath in China in a whisper is something that Chinese have never learned to do, and I felt from the look of complacency on the faces of these men that they did not take half to heart the lecture that I was delivering. If it were possible, however, to express one's feelings in the Chinese language without a howl to be heard half a mile, I must have gotten something of my feelings across to these three aspiring scoundrels. I had to be satisfied with this. I think that these rather unfriendly deliberations were concluded without anyone in the village even suspecting any unpleasantness between members of our little group.

Counting burden-bearers and all, there were sixteen people in the party which left the village at daylight and headed into the densely wooded mountains. I always walked a considerable distance ahead in order to come upon any stray bandits who might be abroad, for should our large party suddenly emerge upon bandits in those mountains, it would immediately be fired upon, so tense had been the atmosphere for months during the struggle between the military and the outlaws.

It seemed to me that the mountains of Fukien were never so beautiful as on that spring morning. I had at last penetrated the deep recesses of the region where virgin forests stood. Rhododendrons vied with azaleas, the latter hanging in gorgeous colors and profusion from trees thirty feet in height. No country could put out a greater wealth of flowering trees and shrubs than we were passing through all forenoon.

As I was topping a heavily wooded divide far ahead of the party I raised my head to see silhouetted against the skyline a long row of bayonets. Barely showing above a low mud barricade was a row of military caps. I knew that I was coming upon a band of bandits, for no soldiers were to be found that far back in the mountain fastness. Who they were, and what they were crouching there for was the question which perplexed me, but it behooved me to get in touch with the armed men before the members of the party following should even see them. Otherwise there might have been both excitement and a stampede. Fortunately, a bend in the trail at this point gave me ample time to do this.

As I approached the waiting bandits without so much as altering my step I thought again of the advice not to undertake the venture of making the trip across the mountains. There was nothing to do now but face the crowd, who were as still as statues silhouetted against the sky. Rounding the end of the low wall I came full upon the men, who, at a command from their leader, arose and saluted me, bringing their guns to rest. The lieutenant in charge of the squad then advanced and handed me a card of greetings from his chief, Dang Gi Ling. A little note was also handed me from the chief saying that he had sent out twenty-six of his picked men to escort our party through a region where there were lurking dangers.

We learned that a band of bandits from the neighboring county, and the country through which the flow of guns and ammunition from the coast had been kept up for months, had been sent out to break up our work of reconciliation, and it was known that we were to be attacked in this particular stretch of mountain fastness. All this added zest to our undertaking, but at the same time assured me that the chief we were going to interview meant business. He was noted for courage and zeal in all things.

It was still a dozen miles to where we would spend the night. We had no opportunity to go through many formalities, for the lieutenant sidled over and held a short conference with the interpreter, who came to me suggesting it would be wise to get out of the heavily wooded area as quickly as possible.

The last lap of the journey was started silently. No one seemed inclined to speak. It was a study of a lifetime to watch these bandits as we wended our way hurriedly along the wooded, winding trail. The last two miles was over the most rugged kind of country, where it several times became necessary to get down on all-fours to climb mere wild animal trails. Five bandits heavily armed kept well ahead, and five with like equipment well in the rear. There seemed but little danger of an attack from the flanks on account of the dense cover. It was a journey fit to kill the less-hardened of the party. I was beginning to feel the strain myself, though I had been scouting over the mountains of the province on foot for many years. The well-fed general and the special deputy from the Tuchün suffered most, for this business was new to them.

Crossing the summit of a high mountain we came upon a basin surrounded by ragged cliffs. This basin had been cleared, and in the center stood a two-story house, with a number of smaller houses scattered around. This was the stronghold of bandit chief Dang. He had chosen this isolated and impregnable spot and built the houses himself. But few people other than bandits so much as knew it was there, and they were those who had been captured and held for ransom. Before any man was released he was bound with an oath of a character effectually to seal his lips forever. No force of soldiers accustomed to the barren hills of the northern provinces would ever venture into such a place. It was as safe as though upon another planet.

A table was spread with many kinds of cakes and dainties, tea and wine, and placed at the further end of a bridge

composed of one slender plank across a deep ravine. Beside this table stood the bandit chief.

As we approached the bridge my interpreter whispered
to me that we were just to sit at the table, but were not
expected to touch even the tea. We were being greeted
with a form of etiquette formerly practiced only when the
emperor was being received. It would be a great mistake, so
my companion assured me, even to touch anything, though
we would be hard pressed by the chief both to eat and drink.

We greeted the bandit, readily taking the seats assigned to us, but soon I bowed low and arose, which was
a sign for all to follow suit. The bandit chief pressed us to
partake of the dainties for a time, then arose and led the
way one hundred yards up the approach to his home.

The house where we were to be entertained was a veri-
table blockhouse. It was a roomy, two-story building, built
to accommodate comfortably, according to Chinese stan-
dards, one hundred or more men. In the center of the
building on the upper floor was a spacious reception hall,
very appropriately decorated for the occasion.

When we entered the hall there was nothing so much
as to suggest that we were in the stronghold of an outlaw.
Handsome banners of satin and silk covered the walls, while
the place was fragrant with bouquets of beautiful mountain flowers. Behind the three chairs set against the wall
in the place of honor hung three large Sabbath-school
scrolls, each portraying some act of Jesus. One could for
the moment more easily imagine himself in a place of
worship than in a building literally alive with outlaws.

I was assigned to the seat of honor, with the others
seated according to the custom of the people. We soon
settled down to business while a feast was being spread
in the center of the hall. I consumed about fifteen minutes making known the object of my coming, and why I

became party to the work in hand, taking especial pains to impress upon all that I meant absolutely fair play. This conversation lasted until eight o'clock when we were invited to take seats around the table. I was asked in a most gracious manner to say grace at the feast table. More and more I became impressed with the fact that things were out of harmony with all for which this place was noted, yet there was an atmosphere of sincerity in it all.

After the saying of grace fifty armed men quietly filed into the room, taking their stand along the wall almost encircling the table. At this juncture the chief requested the privilege of making a few statements. He had so arranged the seating at the table a to place himself opposite the general who had accompanied me. His remarks were rather pointed, and directed at this man.

He began in a courteous manner to discourse upon the strife which had been going on between the soldiers and the bandits, referring in a polite yet sarcastic way to certain battles which had been fought in which the soldiers suffered heavy losses. He pointed out that it was high time that the matter be settled by arbitration, as the bandits could never be suppressed by force, emphasizing the fact that these people were outlaws because it had been forced upon them, and the presence of the northern soldiers in the community had perpetuated it.

The bandit chief drove home the cruelties of the soldiers, reciting instances of ruthless pillaging and burning of whole communities, winding up by saying, "General Wang, you people have within the past months executed more than three thousand people. In all of your cutting off of heads you have not caught ten bandits. In this matter it is impossible that a bandit chief be mistaken." It all was a most terrible arraignment of facts, but no matter how these military men might have felt there was nothing now for them to do but sit patiently under this rapid-fire of accusations.

In closing his speech the chief played a most impressive card. It had, of course, been told him that there was more treachery in this present movement, and that any chief who agreed to meet these men in a parley was courting danger. It was evident that he had implicit confidence in me, but that he felt these men would willingly sacrifice even me upon the altar of their ambitions.

With his keen eyes upon the general, the bandit said, "General Wang, I am called a fool for permitting you to enter my place of abode and sit with me at a feast table. It has been suggested how easy a matter it would be for you to come to my presence with a sleeve gun [pistol] concealed up your sleeve; what an easy matter for you to shoot me dead across the table. As I sit here facing you I realize it would indeed be an easy thing for you to either shoot me above or under the table. But can you fly? Can you suddenly disappear as a spirit does? If you could do neither, you would not live long enough to know whether your shot across or under the table took effect," waving his hand toward the armed men standing sullenly around us.

Here the bandit squared his broad shoulders, and then added: "Well, after all, what is the use of thinking of these things that other men think of? It would be a very great and commendable thing for an outlaw to exchange his life for that of an illustrious officer in the government army. Let us proceed to the discussion of more important matters."

Enough had been said. No matter what might have been in the mind of anyone present, there was now no danger of any attempt at trickery. We sat at the table and feasted and talked until three o'clock in the morning. One wondered where such a bountiful supply of food and dainties could possibly come from in such an out-of-the-way place, many miles from any market.

After we had discussed all the questions brought tip by either side we withdrew from the table, whereupon the chief asked me to retire to his private room for a few moments. Upon taking our seats on his elaborately spread bed he immediately asked me to explain about the guns. Before I could answer he pointedly asked, "Do I understand by this failure to deliver the guns that the government is afraid to trust me?"

The chief then went on to say that he cared nothing about so many guns, pointing out that he could send his men out and catch a certain wealthy farmer from whom he could exact money enough to purchase any number of guns. But then, squaring around on the edge of his bed and looking me in the face, he said, "Mr. Caldwell, I have confidence in you because you are an American and a missionary, but I have neither confidence in, nor respect for, those who have accompanied you. I demanded the guns from the government in order to ascertain whether or not these men are sincere in their desire for peace. With the guns I will agree to terms of peace, but without the definite promise from you that the guns will be forthcoming I will have to bid you good-by with the coming of daylight."

I did not answer any question put to me, but merely said that I myself was greatly concerned over the gun matter, making it plain that my concern was caused by a sense of the responsibility upon the chief in receiving such a number of guns. I impressed upon him what the consequences would be in the event that one of the guns got lost, closing by saying, "Mr. Dang, if you are going to insist upon those guns I am afraid that I cannot become responsible for what might follow, so you had better permit me to step out of the negotiations right where we are, and you can go ahead with the men who promised the sixty guns. There will always be most cordial feelings between you and me."

At this juncture the chief got up and pulled a heavily iron bound trunk from under the bed. From this box he took out a commission furnished him by the mayor of Yuki City appointing him to the high office of commander-in-chief of the constabulary of the county; also a large seal of office. Holding these up he said, "Now I can carry on my work under the name of the government, and I can call the money that I assess the people 'taxes.' I am now in a better position to do business than ever before, and no one can call me a bandit."

Immediately I saw the seriousness of the situation, for what these men had done was actually to endow this bandit with both a commission and a seal with which he could openly conduct any kind of money-grafting career. The men responsible for this blunder dare not report his bad conduct to the higher-ups. It was an awkward position.

The chief then handed me a document promising the sixty guns and sixty thousand rounds of ammunition, definitely stating that I would be responsible for their delivery. My position in the matter was one demanding that I either deliver guns or expose the whole plot, and it would never do to let this man know that I was not a party to the whole deal. My only hope was to barter with the man and get him to weaken in his stand.

I knew full well that it would be impossible for me to deliver even one of the modern military rifles, each of which was registered and had to be accounted for to the Tuchün in Foochow. The general in charge of the bandit affairs even now dreaded the day of reckoning when he would have to account for many guns captured from his soldiers, and those taken by the soldiers who had mutinied and turned bandit. Even to propose to him that he give outright sixty of these guns to the bandits would invite disaster upon the whole affair.

How I would extricate myself from the embarrassing position I found myself now in was a matter of gravest concern, for if I let it be known that I was not a party to the promise of guns, not a man who accompanied me into those mountains would live an hour. My only defense was to play for time.

I argued until daylight trying to get this man to abandon the demands for guns, appealing all the while to his honor in the matter and trying to get him to see how much more dignified it would be to look with utter contempt upon the whole proffer of guns. I wanted the people to know that my friends among the bandits could not be bought and traded for like so many sheep.

I knew that the mayor in Yuki City had hundreds of old obsolete single shot rifles which had never been reported to Foochow, and which were at his disposal. Here was my only hope. In order to get the bandit to accept these guns I had to play long upon his pride. Failing utterly in my endeavors to dispose of the gun matter, I arose from the bed, remarking that it was now daylight, and that I should be on the move.

As I turned to go I said, "It has not appealed to you that your demand for so many guns reflects very great lack of confidence in me. People will interpret it as being an indication of your feeling that you still have to trust to your own prowess. This thing reflects discredit upon me." With these words I walked out of the room.

I had suggested that I would stand for ten of the old single-shot rifles and ten thousand cartridges. The chief hailed me, saying, "Mr. Caldwell, I would not have you for a minute think that I mistrust you. Go ahead and get the ten guns. All I want is to prove that the government is sincere. Tell that general in Yuki, bandit Dang Gi Ling will accept his proffer of ten useless guns instead of sixty that he promised, and say to him that as head of the constabulary of the county I will be responsible not only for the lives of the people of the several townships, but for the lives of the pigs and poultry as well. Tell him no bandit will cross the county boundary to return to tell of deeds of valor he has done."

With this concession on the part of the chief my real troubles had just begun. It was agreed that I proceed to Yuki City, and that I should give a definite reply concerning the ten guns not later than the evening of the third day. This date was fixed by the bandit because his exact whereabouts were known by the military men, and it was possible that an attempt would be made to bottle him up. I left him at an early hour with the definite understanding that if no messenger from me arrived on the evening of the third day, he was to understand that I had failed to secure the ten guns, and he should act accordingly. To gain his confidence I whispered into his ear as we parted, "If my messenger fails to appear on time, my advice would be that you shift your position."

Very much to my surprise I found the escort of twenty-six picked men outside awaiting me. I noticed that they seemed more agitated when we entered the defiles of the forest, but attached no importance to it. When we reached a point near where they had met me the day before two men were sent on far ahead. These men kept their distance well ahead. I was in the middle of the line of march, twelve bandits bringing up the rear. There was much signaling back and forth by whistle and bird calls, but little talking during the first three hours of the march.

As we came into an opening at one point I looked far ahead and saw what I supposed to be one of the large

Atticus atlas moths resting on the top of a reed stalk in a field beside the road. I wanted this specimen very much, but was shocked to see the two leaders rush out and grab the moth roughly in their hands. They called back something in dialect unknown to me, whereupon the lieutenant and two others hurried forward.

Upon reaching the five men standing beside the road examining the catch I saw that it was not a moth at all, but a piece of red paper with a message of some kind written in bold letters. This paper had been placed there by some person who knew we would be passing through, but by whom I never learned; nor did I learn the character of the message other than that it concerned plans of another band of bandits having to do with breaking up the work we were trying to do.

The lieutenant announced to me that he would accompany me clear through to the township. Evidently, there was danger along the route, and these young men had been intrusted with the task of safe conduct. Their actions during the next few hours showed that they meant to make good.

The announcement that these men were going all the way with us, while reassuring in a way, gave rise to one very grave question. Though there was a truce declared during the time of our deliberations, the tension was so great that clashes almost invariably followed a meeting of soldiers and bandits. Each were suspicious of the other, and it was very much a question of who got the first volley in, for the soldiers would generally withdraw after the battle began.

Stationed at the township to which I was going was a large force of soldiers which had had many a clash with these same bandits. I wondered what would happen when these soldiers saw a small force of the bandits, led by the son of the chief, in their very clutches. It worried me. I would have much preferred to have proceeded on my way alone and run any risk of ambush rather than to have these bandits accompany me to the barracks of the soldiers.

A man hurriedly passed us and I hailed him to know where he was going. He was going on to Twenty-fourth Township, he said, so I gave him a message to the officer in charge for the day to the effect that I was bringing out a force of bandits, and that I wanted the soldiers to extend a cordial welcome.

"Be sure to say to the officer that I send word to him that the way these bandits are received will be considered by me as a reception to myself," were my final instructions to the man, who only grunted an inarticulate reply and was gone. I did not so much as know whether or not the man would deliver any message, as all people dreaded going about the soldiers.

As we came down a densely wooded mountain slope to a stream I looked across toward the barracks to see a great stir among the soldiers. No one else seemed to have seen it yet, but as we crossed the stream on an arched bridge the lieutenant in charge of the bandit squad saw the soldiers falling in line. He ordered a quick halt on the bridge, quickly throwing a cartridge into the barrel of his rifle.

There was a clacking of bolts as each gun was loaded. We were crossing the bridge in single file. I was in the middle of the group and just behind the young officer. I touched him on the shoulder saying: "Be at peace and fear nothing from the soldiers. You are now my guests and I am responsible for whatever takes place to-day. If you are fired on, fire first on me for leading you into a trap." Being thus reassured the order was given to march, but I noticed that the guns were not unloaded.

We proceeded to follow the narrow trail winding among the rice fields. I knew that the untimely firing of a firecracker might draw a volley from the nervous bandits. I was under none the less strain now as I did not know what the stir among the soldiers meant. They were now out in force and could be plainly seen getting into formation.

Not until we were within one hundred yards of them did I really relax. It was then that I saw the men were out in side arms only. To thus welcome an armed force was the highest etiquette known. I breathed the first easy breath since the finding of the butterfly early in the day. It was a trying day for me, and I found later that the others shared the same apprehensions that had troubled me.

We had a fine time in the barracks of the soldiers, who went so far as to bring basins of hot water and towels for bathing the hands and feet of the tired bandits. After a good dinner together these men announced that they would return immediately to their chief by another way. I tried to prevail upon them to spend the night with us as it was now near sundown, but the officer suggested that their presence might be needed far back in the hills. I accompanied them to the gate of the village, where they posed for a photograph and then bowed a low adieu. They were soon seen far up the mountain on a trail taking an entirely different direction from the one we had come out. My troubles were not yet over. I started at dawn for Yuki City to render my report to the general-in-charge. At a late hour that evening I had an interview with him in his headquarters. There were with me during the interview the three men who had balled things up by promising the sixty guns. These men did not know what report I would render, but it behooved each to be present to gather laurels in case I reported the private interview with the chief a success.

After brief formalities and considerable tea drinking I announced that the bandit chief had agreed to certain terms, and was now waiting a reply from me. In response to this statement the spectacled general bowed low and drew deep from the yard-long pipe which was constantly fed by an attendant at the other end.

When I announced condition number one the general smiled approval and wrote it down. So it was with number two, three, and four, but when number five was announced thunder and smoke turned loose.

"Ten guns and ammunition!" shouted the goggle-eyed soldier as he brought his huge fist down upon the table, setting all the cups into a merry-go-round dance. He laid down his pen and looked steadily at me for a moment, then struck the table again with his palm, bawling out, "Guns! Do you mean you promised that devil ten guns?"

Everyone in the room was excited now but me, and I would have been afraid had it not been that I was forced to play a certain game regardless of cost. I replied that I had promised ten rifles in working condition with ample ammunition for each, and that unless these should be granted the whole thing would fall through.

"Fall through!" he shouted. "You have already knocked the bottom out of it."

Here the burly brute talked to me as I had never dreamed I would permit any man to talk to me. He called me a "foreign child" who had played with a life-and-death matter as with toys, closing his tirade with these words, uttered half pathetically, half angrily: "You have played the part of a child; you have wrecked my hopes of a settlement of this affair, and now you come asking that I give that bandit guns when he must turn in his guns to me. You may go your way now. I will need your services in this matter no more."

Seldom would a full-blooded American take such a berating from any man and not boil over. I quenched the fire consuming me from within and replied as calmly as I could, "What your honorable self says is all true and strictly in keeping with reason, but the facts remain that there must be ten guns and ammunition, or the whole matter fails."

I assured the enraged general that I had played the fool and all that, and that all the abuses he was heaping upon me were deserved, but as the hour was now late I would retire to let him think it over, assuring him that I must have a reply by the very first peep of dawn. My only request was that he do not wait until he had washed his face in the morning to let me know, as I had promised the chief to have word back by dusk the following day.

As I crossed the threshold I turned and said, "Remember, guns or no guns, the thing will fall through unless you let me know your decision before dawn."

When we were out in the street the three culprits fairly fell upon my neck in tears. The mayor wept aloud, saying, "How kind of you, Mr. Caldwell, to endure all that scolding on account of the blunder we made! Had you spoken but one word of the truth, you could have taken glory to yourself in bartering with the bandits until you had reduced sixty modern rifles down to ten old single-shots. You could easily have saved yourself by exposing us."

The three men were deeply moved by what I had put up with in order to save them from disgrace, declaring that they never once thought that a foreigner would suffer such abuse for the sake of the Chinese. I bowed them a good night and hurried up to the chapel, where I was to sleep.

At midnight there was a call at my door. A man who had come with a message from the general was waiting outside. The message said that the ten guns would be granted and everything carried out in accordance with the conditions laid down by me. I got a man off at daylight with my report to the bandit chief.

Just as I was preparing my message to be hurried through to the bandit the mayor darkened the door of the chapel. He had come over, he declared, because he could not sleep, and he wanted to thank me again for refusing to expose him in what he had done. At the close of a long conversation, he said, "Mr. Caldwell, I want to learn a gospel which will permit men to do what you did."

Since that day the mayor has been a frequent attendant at religious services in our church. I cannot even estimate what amount of the "doctrine" has sunken through the crust of the man, but that he has heard a lot of preaching of the gospel since that night in the general's yamen is certain. He counts himself still a "learner."

I handled the matter of the transfer of the ten guns to the bandits, trying the action of every rifle in order to see that not even a little thing like a broken spring in an obsolete gun could hinder the matter of closing up this business. I had been through too much already to permit any little thing like that to prove a hitch.

When this was done I started to my boat, calling in to say good-by to the general. I did not even sit down to have the customary cup of tea, but after a word or so of greeting said, "General Chang, you did not understand why I demanded ten guns, but you will understand some day. On that day you will realize how difficult it is for an American missionary who really loves China to do anything for the country. I assure you that I did the best I could."

I turned to hurry away, when the burly palm was laid upon my shoulder. I turned to look straight into the eyes of the general. His palm slipped from my shoulder slowly down my arm until the big hand clasped mine tightly.

"Ah, my friend, I realize now who it was played the fool. How could you possibly endure my harsh words in order to save the guilty ones? It is all over now, but I want to apologize for the unkind things that I said to you." The man broke into a sob, and we parted, each with eyes dimmed by tears.

XIV

More Bandits

One can hardly think of outlaws dispensing law, but I actually found these chiefs holding court, trying cases, and dispensing justice. One chief I visited held regular courts in order that the people, who could get no semblance of justice in the regular courts, because they could not engage the necessary influential scholar or play lawyer for them, could get fair play.

The so-called lawyer of the old school cared nothing about interpretation of law, for his whole object was to pervert justice, and to keep cases as far as possible from an adjustment according to the merit of testimony in courts. His greatest source of income was in playing the part of a middleman in arbitrating cases outside the court. If business was lacking, he had means of creating it.

I recall one instance when, during a siege of bubonic plague, a man died beside the road near my home. It was upon material of this kind that the lawyer thrived, so immediately a scholar noted for his daring instigated trouble, urging the relatives of the dead man to take the corpse by night and lay it at the door of a wealthy member of a rival clan. Murder charges followed, in which this noted lawyer directed the matter of framing the charges. Rather than have the matter enter the courts supported by a man of reputation of this lawyer, the accused asked that it be adjusted by arbitration. The lawyer fixed five thousand

dollars as the price upon which the case would be com-
promised, putting the lion's share of the spoils in his
pocket.

Realizing how impossible it was for the poor people to
get justice where the scholar of the old school was playing lawyer, these bandit chiefs often held courts in which
all kinds of difficulties were adjudged and adjusted. No
one dare go counter to the decision of such a judge. In all
such instances where I had occasion to investigate I
learned of no case where the bandit acted counter to the
merits of the testimony given. Notwithstanding the terrible
suffering caused by the presence of so many bandits
abroad, one often heard the people expressing a prefer-
ence for the bandit courts to the regular tribunals. Never
once did I hear a suggestion of bribery entering into a
decision by a bandit judge.

I passed through one township which a few days previously had been visited by a band of northern soldiers.
The soldiers had burned the homes of two families because
the bandits in passing through had rested a few hours
there, cooking their own dinner in the kitchens of the
homes. The bandits realized that they had forced their
presence upon these homes, and consequently realized
that they were suffering on account of no offense of their
own. After the soldiers withdrew from the community the
chief sent some of his best men down to investigate the
matter and to appraise the property destroyed. He accepted without question the valuation placed upon the
property by his representatives, reimbursing both families
fully for the loss they had sustained.

The bands of bandits operate in definite areas which
have been agreed upon among themselves, and it is a
breach of both etiquette and faith for one band to operate
in the territory of another. Death was the inevitable end
of the bandit who was found guilty of a violation of this
rule.

Among other unwritten laws was that which made a person exempt from further assessment after once paying a ransom for release. That is to say, such an individual could not be captured a second time after holding a receipt from a bandit chief for a payment to purchase his freedom. If some so-called "wild bandit" undertook to use the name of a dreaded chief operating in an area and extorted money from one who had already paid in the regular way, the death penalty was immediately fixed for the offender, and he was sure to die at the hands of a bandit sooner or later.

Practically every well-to-do family residing in the area where a force of bandits has operated for any considerable length of time has been reduced to abject poverty. This has been due to the multiplicity of taxes on account of the bandit personnel changing so often, and on account of the constant extortion practiced by the soldiers.

The bandits are most exacting in their discipline, and one seldom hears of a breach of faith under orders from a recognized chief. I saw one city which had been taken by the bandits placarded throughout streets and alleys with the rules of occupation. Among other most commendable rules were a number affixing the death penalty upon any bandit who insulted a woman, looted a shop, or desecrated a Christian chapel or school. These men were bandits by force of circumstances other than by chance. One only has to see these outlaws actually in action in order to appreciate what the character of many of the men must have been before they were forced into such a life. After I completed my work with chief Dang Gi Ling there was a period of a few weeks when I was spared having to devote much time or attention to this kind of work. I had hoped the impulse given the movement would prompt all other chiefs to follow suit and come to terms with military authorities along the lines we had laid down, but such was not to be the case.

Not one of these men would so much as meet the deputies and military men for a parley until I would in person or by proxy "nod my head," as they called it, thus becoming sponsor for the deliberations and responsible for all consequences. I was, of course, very careful to maintain a very stiff neck in all matters which I did not personally negotiate. The facts are that I had just as little confidence in the military men as the bandits did, knowing that, with the possible exception of one man, they would willingly sacrifice both me and the church in order to get promotion.

This one man became very much attached to me. I never once had occasion to criticize him during a period of several months' work with him. One day I received a communication by special messenger from him saying that if I could arrange to be at a certain place on a given day, Chief Cong Cu Hung would meet me. There was a terrible flood in the river and even the mail boats were not running, but in order for me to meet this man at the time and place agreed upon a thirty-three-mile trip down the rapids and then about as far across the mountains was required.

I found a boatman who agreed to undertake to get me down the river. I will not forget that day, when our lone little boat was as a bit of driftwood on the beating current of the river, but as we were being swept along at the rate of twelve miles an hour I found consolation in the fact that it would not take us long to get to our landing point.

It was pouring rain when the boat pulled up to the shore by a lonely village. The securing of burden-bearers required an hour or more, rendering it unpleasantly late when we struck inland for the long journey.

When we reached the village agreed upon I found my faithful military friend awaiting me. He expressed great surprise upon seeing me come into the village, and exclaimed, "I might have known that you would come, even though everyone did say you could not possibly get down the river." Before even changing my clothes or taking a cup of tea I hurried a runner off with my card to ascertain whether or not the bandit was waiting for me at the trysting place three miles further inland.

I made bold to invite the chief down to the village to spend the night as my guest, little believing that he would dare accept the invitation, but, sure enough, he returned with my messenger. This one expression of confidence assured the success of my undertaking. After sitting up until a late hour discussing matters I retired feeling well repaid for the hard trip of the day.

On the following morning the chief led our party back into the mountains, where his entire force of bandits were awaiting us. Negotiations moved rapidly, as I found that practically every one of these sturdy young men was anxious to return to his home. One thing, however, finally threatened to wholly block the deliberations. Four of the bandits had but a week before purchased rifles and ammunition from some agency getting the supplies from Japanese sources, paying one thousand dollars apiece for the guns, and one dollar for each cartridge. They refused to sacrifice this amount of money, demanding that they be reimbursed for their financial outlay.

This raised a very serious question. To sell the guns to the military meant a loss of face on the part of the bandits; while to buy them meant the same for the general acting with me. To be either forced to sell or forced to buy looked bad, from whatever angle the transaction was viewed.

There remained but one thing for me to do, and that was to offer "to buy" the guns myself. So, after consulting the general, I put the proposition up to the bandits, assuring them that while I had good guns of my own for big game shooting I might be able to use their guns. They readily understood the deal and knew full well who was putting up the money for the purchase of the guns, but their "faces" were saved. The deal went through with neither guns nor money passing through my hands. This was a necessary step in the negotiation.

Now that the negotiations were completed, the entire band of armed men accompanied me down to the village. We had arranged to entertain them in the only two-story house in the place, which was just across the street from the building I was occupying. Quantities of fresh straw were provided so that the men might sleep in comfort, while under the building were other bales of straw upon which they could draw.

I was very much pleased with the arrangements which had been made by the elders of the village, but too much straw and too much comfort did not appeal favorably to the always suspicious bandits. One of the bandits suggested that the presence of so much fresh straw under the house and on both floors would make it an easy and quick matter to burn the place and trap them all alive. Like a herd of frightened sheep the whole band bolted out of the house, creating a commotion throughout the community.

We all rushed out to see what was the matter, and found these armed men grouping in strategic places ready for action. It was a critical moment, but we soon had things pretty well quieted down, though do what we could we were not able to get the bandits to reenter the building.

The proposition now resolved itself into one of having several hundred bandits in the village with no place to entertain them or getting a new place. The only possible solution of the question was to turn to the ancestral hall, knowing that such a move would go far toward restoring confidence.

Within less than an hour we were all occupying this large building, borrowing beds, bedding, and cooking utensils from all parts of the village. To make everyone feel perfectly at ease I ordered my load moved over, and my cot set up in the midst of the central room occupied by the bandits. While every man seemed to be quite at ease, there was not a man of the more than one hundred sleeping in the room with me who as much as removed his cartridge belt during the night. Each man slept with his gun beside him, and his sandals on.

The following day was given up to the matter of details— issuing of pardons, turning in of guns, and so on. The last act of Chief Cong Cu Hung as a bandit was to place his large seal upon no less than one hundred proclamations which had been written during the day, announcing his disbanding of the bandits and his and their return to citizenship. This document called upon any person finding any man using his name or influence in connection with the collecting of "taxes" or extorting money to arrest the guilty party and turn him over to the military authorities to be put to death.

After affixing his signature and seal to these documents the bandit turned to me with these words: "Teacher, I have nothing to bestow upon you to express to you my gratitude for your kindness in paving the way for me and my men to return to our homes, but take this," handing me his large seal, "and hold it, knowing that it will never again be used in the abuse of the rights of the people."

This is the man referred to in another chapter as having been accused by some gentry of buying rice for the bandits, at which time he was arrested, his ancestral home burned, and his father and mother brutally murdered, his own life being saved only when the elders of several scores of villages went security. He had, during the intervening years, wreaked terrible vengeance upon his enemies until his soul was satisfied. Now he was ready to lay down his arms and return to quiet life.

Within one week from the day I parted with him he went in person to Foochow to express his regrets to the Tuchün for having violated the laws of the land. He was a desperate man as a bandit chief, and he was desperately in earnest when he gave up the life of an outlaw. The military governor was so impressed by his character that he spread a great feast for him, and called in a troop of actors to stage a special theater play in his honor. Later, he was urged by the Tuchün to take charge of his personal bodyguard, a position he held for three years with marked distinction. He is now living a quiet life in a market town on the river one hundred miles above Foochow.

There now remained two large forces of bandits to be brought to terms, and I had but a few weeks remaining until I was due to start for America to engage in a special missionary campaign. Some busybodies took advantage of the situation and started a report to the effect that I was given two months by the Chinese government to clean up the bandit business, since I was engaged for that purpose on a ten-thousand-dollar salary, failing which I was to be deported. They reported that my job was to deceive the bandits to the point that they could all be trapped and executed.

While these reports were extravagant to the point of being ridiculous, still they had a noticeable reaction upon the bandits, both among many who had already returned to their homes and those whom I hoped yet to bring to terms. One chief refused outright to see me under any conditions. The reasons for this refusal were very evident.

It was exceedingly important that I see Chief Ding Cu Geng, the most notorious, most suspicious, and most powerful of all. As I began to get in touch with him other influences began to make themselves felt. Representatives from certain of these interests waited upon him assuring him that a movement was on to trap him. I met a man from Canton who was delegated to offer him the tuchünship of the province if he would but lead in a great movement to overthrow the then provincial power.

Possibly that which hindered most was the report conveyed to him by supposedly trustworthy parties that I was working for wages, and that, while I was responsible to the bandits there would be no treachery, I was secretly packing up to leave the country as soon as I could turn the bandits bodily into the power of the military authorities. These are but samples of what I was confronted with in my efforts to get an interview with this chief.

At this particular time there was a Japanese medicine peddler who was very active throughout the region. I came up against his influence everywhere. His worst crime seemed to be the injecting of drugs into ex-opium addicts at ten cents an injection, but the facts were that he was behind some powerful move to prevent Ding Cu Geng coming to terms, or even meeting me. I encountered his influence in a very direct way more than once during the last weeks of my work with the bandits.

Ding Cu Geng could well afford to give up this life as an outlaw leader. True, he had been provoked to take up this life, and to continue it as none other that I had met. Crimes against this man, his personal family, and his clan by the soldiers were of a character to prompt him to follow them to the brink of the great abyss in order to take revenge. At one time a band of soldiers, led by an officer who had repeatedly been beaten and chagrined by this powerful chief, attacked the ancestral tombs of the Ding clan, wrecking the graves and beating the bones into powder.

This greatest of all offenses followed a few weeks upon the murder of the chief's mother, when the soldiers tied her to a tree and killed her by the method known as "a thousand cuts," meaning that the victim would have one thousand bits of flesh snipped off by the executioners' sword before life passed out of the body. Bent upon revenge, the name of this chief became one before which soldiers quaked.

When pressed too hard by an overwhelming force of soldiers with quick-firing guns, he would retreat to the great forest known as "Mi Gu Lang," from whence he would hurl defiance at his foe. No soldier who ever entered that forest returned to his friends alive. Several who dared to venture in after the chief were sent out in a rude pine box as a gift to the officer in charge of the attacking squad. Robin Hood at his best never excelled this man in banditry, who by this time had wealth enough buried in the hills to purchase a whole county.

Suspicion was the undoing of the man. He was suspicious of his best friends, placing implicit confidence in no one. When he buried loot in the hills he sealed the treasures in a manner all his own. He never took more than two men with him, always only one unless the load of silver was too much for a single man. After the treasure was securely buried he returned to the band by some circuitous route, always killing the man or men who had accompanied him on this errand. He died later by accident at the hands of his own men, and to-day his family are living in poverty while his millions tarnish in the hills.

I finally met this man under most peculiar circumstances. It was during the month of August, when the weather is the most trying on account of heat and humidity. We were spending the month in the wooded hills two hours from our station when I received a letter from General Wang saying that he thought that I could see the noted chief if I could come down at once, and could give him satisfactory assurance that there would be no foul play. He informed me that word had been spread by the medicine peddler that there was a move on foot to have eight hundred soldiers intercept the chief if he ventured out to meet me, but that he felt sure that I would find some way to get around the difficulty.

I now knew absolutely that all danger of treachery on the part of the military was over, for I had several "big sticks" which I held heavily over their heads. I knew too that there was but one guarantee that I could give Chief Ding that would insure an interview, for I had been assured as much. But as a father I hesitated to offer my oldest son upon such an altar.

The remaining chief, Lu Hing Bang, had written me assuring me that he would immediately lay down arms upon any conditions Ding Cu Geng would accept. It seemed that there was a fair chance to utterly stamp out brigandage on the whole Yuki field. I decided to undertake to effect a connection with the noted outlaw.

On the following day I started on this important mission, taking with me my son, Oliver, at that time twelve years old. A second invitation was never necessary to get this lad to go with me on any jaunt, but I am not sure but that he would have hesitated on this trip had he understood fully what his going meant. When I said that I was going to take him to see a bandit chief it seemed too good to the lad to be true.

Together we traveled by boat sixty miles down river to a point where I was to meet General Wang. I found him waiting for me with the latest news concerning developments. It seemed very improbable that we would be able to meet the chief, though we all agreed that an effort to do so was more than justified. I did not mention even to the general what I had in mind doing. Only my interpreter for the day, who happened to be one of my most trusted ministers, was let into the secret.

We were to go inland fifteen miles to a certain village, from which point we would undertake to connect up with the bandit. I felt certain that if I could actually get in touch with the chief from that point, that I had a card which I could play insuring me an interview. Accordingly, I sent a messenger two hours ahead of the party to announce to the chief that I would arrive at the village at eleven o'clock, and that as I had the "guarantee" he insisted upon, I would expect him to meet me.

When we reached the village there was not the slightest sign of a bandit in the whole neighborhood. I saw, however, hanging in a hall two bushel baskets of fire-crackers, a half hog, a bundle of pickled ducks, vegetables, and so on. All the indications were that a high-grade feast was looming above the horizon. I felt that no one but the bandit would make such an elaborate spread, and took hope.

Ere long a slovenly-looking fellow slouched around the corner of the building we were occupying. He stood in the door watching us drinking tea. He looked no different from any one of the score of loafers to be found hanging around were there was to be any excitement, and it goes without saying that there was excitement enough in this little community upon having foreigners enter at the head of a procession of men bent upon a mission such as ours was known to be.

I was now ready for almost anything, and was there-fore not surprised to learn that this was one of the bandit chief's most trusted men. He had come to ascertain exactly what our presence meant, and incidentally to say that the chief could not meet me on account of the threatened treachery and the danger of being trapped. I was ready for this, and after all argument was without avail I offered my son as ransom for the day, as a guarantee that there would be no force of soldiers sent out from Yuki City to intercept the bandits.

"Go back and tell the chief that I have brought with me my heir," I told him, "whom I willingly turn over to him as hostage during the interview. If there is any foul play to-day my son is in his hands." The man made a low bow and was soon lost in the forest back of the village.

I waited anxiously for half an hour, almost hoping that the chief would refuse to meet me, for I felt that I had given assurance of good faith and would be able to inter-view him another day. I feared only one thing, and that was that a squad of soldiers traveling from one township to another might possibly come upon Chief Ding's men in wait-ing during the interview. We had agreed that all movement of troops should stop during the days of deliberations, lest there might be clashes, but up to this time these orders had not always been obeyed.

Suddenly and without warning the chief, accompanied by a force of heavily armed men, appeared before the door of the building. Both he and his men seemed unconcerned as we arose to greet him. I turned my boy over to ten of the finest young bandits that I had ever seen, saying, "You run on and play with these young men while I talk with the bandit chief." Each man was armed with both a rifle and one or a brace of pistols, and three of the group had bags of high explosive bombs. The boy did not once suspect what it all meant, nor did he nor his mother know what I had done until two years later, when we were enjoying a furlough in the homeland.

The hours spent in deliberating with the chief were, of course, more or less filled with anxiety, for I did not know what might possibly happen to suggest to the suspicious man treachery, though I felt reasonably secure.

As I conducted my conference with the bandit I saw now and again my son moving around happily with the ten picked men. They were very attentive to him, showing their guns and pistols, and even explaining the working of the bombs.

It was amusing to me later to learn of these bombs. They were made by mixing equal parts of two chemicals, one of which was white and the other bright yellow. The chemicals were purchased, so I was told, through the agency of the Japanese medicine man for a fabulous price. The bandits were told that the white powder was silver powder and the yellow gold powder, the concentration of which two metals produced an explosive stronger than anything else in the world.

The chief took great pride in demonstrating to me the effectiveness of this explosive, which he implicitly believed was concentrated silver and gold. I saw him take a small pinch of each and carefully mix them and lay the compound on a piece of paper which was placed on the door-sill of the house. He then took a heavy stone cutter's hammer and struck the powder, whereupon the hammer was blown from his hand, and the paper shredded into bits.

These bombs were generally used on account of their terrific wrecking power rather than for the killing of people. An attack upon a barracks was always preceded by the throwing of one or more of the bombs against the heavily barred doors. The concussion was such as to wreck the whole front of the building and start a panic among the soldiers within. The soldiers seldom offered any defense where an attack was accompanied by the use of these bombs.

In the early stages of brigandage the bandits would resort to almost any means in order to secure arms and ammunition. Until guns were obtained in sufficient numbers the bandits had to evade the soldiers as far as possible. They then used wooden guns in their work among the villagers, intimidating a community they were attacking by firing a volley of firecrackers behind it. Following this a number of "armed men" would approach the town with guns ready for action. One or two would advance, carrying the card of the bandit chief, and in his name the community would be assessed a large sum of money, and be given an hour in which to pay up in full. A long line of bandits armed with guns made of wood and painted black were standing ready to open fire upon the homes of the village if they refused to produce the amount of tax assessed.

The people of Ninth Township, Yuki, were delivering a huge sum of money to emissaries of the noted chief Lu Hing Bang, when a certain few of the ruffians of the township conceived the idea that this was some kind of a bluff game, whereupon they intercepted the bearers, capturing the thirty thousand dollars and appropriating it to their own use. This thing was reported to the chief. The following morning, at an hour before dawn, he attacked the township with one thousand men, who were ordered to kill and burn indiscriminately. More than three hundred homes were burned and hundreds of people slaughtered regardless of age or sex. This thing was then placarded as an object lesson to any community, which might dare defy the order of a bandit chief.

A boat on the river refusing to pay a tax or assessment fixed by the bandits is sure to come to early grief. The bandits wait an opportunity, whereupon they come down and touch a torch to both boat and cargo, always refraining from appropriating anything on the boat. If the offense has been of a flagrant character, the crew of the ill-fated boat is shot and thrown into the burning cargo. This thing is generally done at a point where many boats are tied up for the night, in order that the others may get the full benefit of the lesson. Other unoffending boats are not molested. The bandits claim this lesson must be given at intervals in order to facilitate the matter of negotiating for "collections" and "taxes."

I succeeded in negotiating a satisfactory deal with Chief Ding, which carried a great promise for the abolition of brigandage in the upper Fukien region.

In fact, it was one of the most satisfactory interviews that I had ever had, and it was with a considerable feeling of relief that I started upon the return trip by moonlight with my boy. I was glad the whole thing was over, for it had been a day of suspense. My boy was enthusiastic over the young men who had attended him all day so attentively, declaring that they did not leave him alone for a minute! It moved my heart to hear the lad talk so, but I comforted myself in the thought that what I had done was for the suffering people of the bandit-infested area. It seemed that I could now see the day when all this disorder would be a thing of the past.

The chief came from his strongholds the following day and spent many days in the barracks of the soldiers on

the river at the head of steam navigation, where conference after conference was held concerning the details in
connection with the final adjustment of the whole bandit
business. Everything moved along speedily, with all concerned entertaining high hopes of a quick return of quiet
and peace throughout the region.

Suddenly a medicine peddler appeared in the community disposing of his wares and carrying on his business.
He even entered the barracks of the soldiers and the headquarters of the officers. No one to this day knows exactly
what happened, but the following morning Ding Cu Geng
was gone. When again heard from he was at the head of a
strong force of bandits which he had quickly organized.
Never again would he listen to any talk of reconciliation.
He had been told something by the traveling doctor which
had suddenly changed him into a raving lion. He wrote
me a most appreciative letter thanking me for all that I
had done in the interest of peace, expressing implicit confidence in me, and apologizing for what he had done. He
assured me that his actions were wholly justified, however,
as the preservation of life was the recognized first law of
being.

This man conducted a ruthless crusade against all his
enemies for a period of more than a year. He even turned
against his former associates who had returned to citizenship, forcing them either to fight or break faith. His attitude
toward these well-meaning people placed hundreds in an
awkward position. Because former Chief Dang Gi Ling
refused to comply with these demands he swore he would
kill him. One night he ambushed the man as he was returning to his home by moonlight, killing the ten armed
guards traveling with him. He carried on this campaign
until his own end came in a strange but most appropriate
manner.

With a force of his men he had surrounded one of the
stockades, or refuges, such as had sprung up all over the

disturbed area, and in which both soldiers and civilians sought refuge. After subjecting the stockade to heavy bombardment he touched the torch. Every possible exit was soon aflame and any moving object was shot at sight.

For some reason the chief crept up to examine one of the burning exits. His men did not see him advance, but caught sight of him in a crouched position as he retreated. True to orders they opened fire upon him, killing him instantly.

An attempt was made in 1920 to trap Lu Hing Bang and his men. He and his men were pardoned by the Tuchün in Foochow, and he was commissioned commander-in-chief of the gendarmerie of the whole Yuki region. He erected a block-house in the Sixth Township which he occupied himself with a picked guard, while his men moved throughout the area preserving order.

In a very few weeks this man established a form of commendable government. All was going well, but the man was no fool. He had been to school in the early days under his chief, Ding Cu Geng, and had learned to trust no man. He lived literally with his ear to the ground. He sent me word that I should not think that he had lost all his senses in that he should become "reconciled" through the offer made by the Tuchün, when he had refused so many times to see me during those days of earnest and honest effort to establish peace.

The chief's adviser had received a gunshot wound in the arm from which he suffered for many months. Some person suggested that he proceed to Yenping and let our missionary doctors look at the arm. He interviewed the chief and asked his advice. The chief replied, "You are taking your own life in your hands by going, even though you are traveling under guarantee of safe conduct. I would not trust the Tuchün nor any of his men one minute. Remember that there is now no missionary going our security. We may expect treachery at any turn of the way. If you think your life is more in danger from your wound than by traveling the road to Yenping you should go. But my advice would be to get the missionary doctor to come to see you here."

The man disregarded the advice given, proceeding to Yenping. He held credentials from the military governor in Foochow, as well as a commission from him. He really should have been safe. Upon reaching Yenping he sent in his card to the general in charge in the city, as well as one to the missionary doctor. The general immediately invited him to come into his yamen and be his guest during his sojourn in the city. He accepted the hospitality, and was executed a few hours later.

Lu Hing Bang heard of this and simply said, "I told him to be careful." As a protest against such actions he sent a large force of his best men to Yuki City, where they ousted the northern troops and took over the command of the city.

The commander of the Yuki City troops called upon me at my home in Yenping, earnestly requesting me to proceed to Yuki to ask the bandit chief to withdraw his men. I had not been traveling that area with my eyes blinded. I had long felt that the bandits were, in a quiet way, being surrounded by troops from other branches of the river.

Upon being hard pressed by the commander to go on this mission for him I looked him squarely in the eye, saying, "General, if I read aright the signs of the times, there is a deep laid plan to entrap Chief Lu Hing Bang, and the moving of his men into Yuki City only delays the thing a little. I prefer to be spared the playing of any part in the matter."

The soldier looked at me with open mouth, exclaiming, "Who told you? How do you know?"

I replied to this man that the plan was a good one, but that I knew enough about the bandit to know that he was no fool, and predicted that the whole scheme would not only fail, but that the bandits would whip the soldiers to a frazzle any time the clash came. Within three days from that time the clash did come, but the bandit who had kept his ear to the ground was ready. He cut his way through the cordon of troops which had been thrown around him and once more took refuge in the hills.

I have never once known the bandits to break faith, though in all their dealings with the military they expect them to play false. Chief Cong Cu Hung had to fight three battles with northern troops in order to meet me at the time and place agreed upon, but he was there on time. My work with them is done, but I shall always think of them as being men possessed with bold daring and ruled with discipline.

XV

"They Saved the City"

The title of this chapter is rather high sounding, but it is not mine. It is what a few tens of thousands of people far up among the mountains said about the conduct of four Americans during what was called in Fukien province the "Third Revolution."

Yuan Shi Kai had just closed his monarchist coup by dying, but the news had not traveled fast enough to thwart the plans of the "republicans" to gain control of Yenping City, which is considered by strategists to be the key to the richest of China's southern provinces.

Always any program for taking this province from the party in power includes first capturing Yenping City, the mere turning of which key can completely shut off the rice supply from Foochow, thus insuring a bloodless taking of that city. Yenping is the key to the province only in the sense that, as it is situated at the juncture of the two main branches of the Min River, one hundred and twenty miles above the capital, the party in control can shut off food supplies, provided it has military strength enough to make good its purpose.

In the attack upon Yenping City there were two factors upon which the success of the enterprise hung. In the first place, the support of the noted bandit chief Ding Cu Geng, about whom much has been said in another chapter, was relied upon, and this man never failed to carry

out any part of a program to which he had definitely committed himself. He was to attack the city under cover of
darkness, directing his attack against the so-called northern
troops occupying the downtown barracks.

In the second place, the southern, or Hunan, troops
occupying the barracks on the hill near the Methodist
hospital compound were relied upon to unite with the "repub-
lican forces," all of whom would strike after the bandits
had forced an entrance into the city. The whole thing had
been worked out in the minutest detail by revolutionist
emissaries who had filtered into the city under one guise
or another.

On Saturday there was given in our mission compound
a lawn party of a purely social nature to which many
prominent Chinese of the city were invited. Among them,
we later learned, were a number of the leading revolutionists. These guests asked to withdraw early upon pretense of
having some very urgent business. They certainly did have
urgent business, for the attack upon the city was to be
begun by the bandits at one hour before daylight the following morning.

Rifle fire broke loose at four o'clock in the morning
along the river front, concentrating around the city gates.
Within less than two hours the city was completely in the
hands of the bandits, and the streets were placarded with
proclamations calling for perfect order.

In the early forenoon I went down on the streets with
another missionary to find the bandits in possession of
everything, standing or loitering around in groups in a
listless manner. The chief was an exceedingly busy man,
however, seeming to be about the only man in the town
who manifested a real interest in the event of the day.

It was very manifest to us that the Hunan, or so-called
southern forces, were not deeply committed to what the
bandits had in hand, manifesting but little interest in
matters of organization of the new city administration.

Their attitude alone was enough to fill us with apprehension. The situation was such as to produce a feeling of unpleasant uncertainty to any interested observer, but the reason for this did not appear on the surface. The outstanding impression was the perfect order maintained by the bandits.

In order to get a better idea of the true situation we made a round of the several yamens on a tour of courtesy calls, extending greetings to the new incumbents in office. This was the proper thing for us to do, of course. Yet we had another purpose. It was important that we find out the exact situation, as rumors were rampant and disquieting, the most disquieting being that a large force of northern soldiers were marching against the city.

Mr. and Mrs. Roy Chapman Andrews, of New York, were our guests at the time, but were spending a few days at a small monastery several hours distant from the city, collecting small mammals for the institution they represented. The serious nature of the attack upon the city was evident and my first thought was of plans for getting our guests back into the city before the gates were closed as a measure of defense. And, too, it might be that we would need the courage and marksmanship of a man like Mr. Andrews in the event riot broke out.

We visited the office of the mayor, finding that chair filled by an indifferent-looking fellow who had been assigned to his incumbency. He was one of those subtle fellows whose very presence is enough to impart an uncanny feeling of insecurity. A few minutes in his presence made us ill at ease. His agitated yet noncommittal attitude showed plainly that the situation was anything but secure. He was one of the leading spirits in the revolution, yet he was trying to maintain an attitude which would serve him in the event the northern troops did actually storm and retake the city.

A visit to the telegraph office revealed nothing other than that the administration had been taken over by the new regime. The fact that code messages were accepted showed that there was no severe censorship. There were a number of English missionaries stationed at Kienning, and we felt it our duty to keep them informed as to the actual situation, since there was a great stir among the twelve hundred Hunan soldiers in that city who were being held in reserve in the event the northerners attacked our city.

After visiting all the public offices we wound up by calling upon the *taotai*, in whom we had implicit confidence. We felt confident that we would learn from this man all that there was to be known if we could have a few minutes conversation with him alone, as he was bitterly opposed to the monarchist movement in the north.

Upper Fukien was already suffering from the hordes of northern soldiers whom the would-be monarch had hurried south to bolster him up in his ambitious move. These men have ever been a curse to the province, and will be so long as they are permitted to roam around imposing all kinds of abuses upon the helpless people.

We found the *taotai* a very worn and haggard man. We inquired of him of what illness had he been suffering, only to find that it was all due to worry over the situation. With a wave of the hand he bade us be seated, exclaiming, "Ah, friends, I am sick with anxiety for my country and my people."

He then discussed with us frankly the local situation, confirming the report that a large force of northern troops were marching up river, and were due to arrive the following day. He predicted that a clash with subsequent looting would follow, since the Hunan men had openly identified themselves with the revolutionists and bandits. He concluded with these words, "This whole thing hangs like a collar around my neck, even though I had nothing to do with it. I am not responsible for the movement which hoisted the revolutionists' flag upon my flagstaff. I very heartily endorse any movement to establish a real republic in China, but deplore this untimely local movement."

The *taotai* pointed out that he had told the revolutionists that Yuan Shi Kai was dead, and urged upon them the futility of starting any revolutionary movement in Fukien as the pretext for the whole uprising had been removed by the death of the would-be monarch. But the weasel-eyed mayor had encouraged the attack upon the city in order to create a disturbance of sufficient magnitude to justify an attack upon the city by the northern soldiers. No matter what the outcome, he was prepared to discredit the *taotai*, who would probably be put to death. The mayor counted upon taking the vacant office, whether northerners or republicans were victorious.

Here the *taotai* broke down and wept, saying: "Well, if the northern soldiers actually enter the city, I will surely have to die, as the flag of the ill-timed movement hangs over my head. I would gladly die if by so doing I could hasten the day of peace in my country, but I am sorry to be accused of being connected with such an ill-advised cause."

Before leaving we advised the *taotai* to try to save himself by hiding in the city, and even discussed with him the safest refuge. Certain mission property was suggested by an interested friend of the unhappy man, but we discouraged this for what we considered very good reasons. A hiding place was finally agreed upon, whereupon we hurried back to our homes upon the hill.

Half an hour later we were standing in front of my door discussing the situation when heavy rifle fire broke loose in different parts of the city, where a few hours before we had found everything perfectly in order under patrol of bandit forces. After a moment's reflection it was evident to all of us that there could be but one explanation, since the balls whizzing overhead were those of modern military weapons. We surmised that the Hunan men had turned upon the bandits in order to be able to save themselves in the event that the northerners attacked in force.

An hour later we again visited the streets to find that our suppositions had been true. The soldiers claimed that the only thing they could do in order to justify their position in what was now a very complicated matter and a lost cause was to turn upon the bandits and clean them out of the city before the northern soldiers arrived. This they had tried to do.

It had been arranged that small groups of soldiers should loiter along the streets, fraternizing with the bandits who were patroling the city. At a certain hour and minute each soldier was to shoot down a bandit, and then press home the advantage thus gained until the street should be pretty well cleared. It was the framing of this dastardly plan that had made the newly appointed mayor so ill at ease during our visit in the forenoon.

After the first attack upon the bandits the soldiers were to take over the city and begin a campaign of rounding up both bandits and revolutionists. Intrigue and treachery of this nature is frequent in China where the military is involved.

The man hunt was being carried on unrelentingly by the Hunan men, their only hope of saving themselves being to avoid a clash with the northerners now nearing the city, armed with a number of rapid-fire guns. The Hunanese counted much on being able to show a big bag of captured bandits and revolutionists, as well as a great many dead upon the streets of the city, as evidence of their good faith and prowess. As it developed later, our own use of the latter evidence went far toward averting a serious clash between the two bodies of soldiers.

In the afternoon we organized a bit of Red-Cross force and began to look up the wounded still suffering unnoticed on the streets of the city. I divided a scarlet necktie with Mr. Andrews. Tying this around our arms, and attended by a couple of stretcher-bearers with a stretcher furnished by the mission hospital, we set out for the street. Soon the wounded began to arrive at the hospital, where Dr. Trimble and his assistants became swamped with work. They worked for hours without a breathing spell, tackling even the most serious cases with a coolness and skill which would do credit to any surgeon surrounded by every possible help and convenience in a fully equipped hospital in the homeland.

If crosses and decorations were awarded to all who deserve them, Dr. Trimble most certainly would have received both in recognition of his services for the suffering on that and the following day.

At dusk a dear Chinese friend of mine, whom I had not seen for a number of days, came to my home looking as though he had been ill for weeks. The poor man recited the ordeal through which he had passed with much feeling. What he told me was enough not only to reflect light upon what he had been through, but upon his Christian character as well.

At the time of the attack by the soldiers upon the bandits he was on the streets, narrowly escaping death several times during the fusillade. Upon reaching home he found two strangers sitting in his reception hall. These men introduced themselves as being prominent revolutionists who had fled into his home, being chased by soldiers. While he was explaining to them the danger to himself and family through their presence there was a tapping at the door, followed by a figure hurriedly crowding in. This was the bandit chief, Ding Cu Geng.

The situation now became alarmingly serious for my friend and his family, for had these men been found in the house the whole family would probably have been executed. The fugitives begged to be allowed to remain in the home, finally refusing to move into the open until nightfall. The city gates had been carefully guarded so that it was known that these men were still in the city, where a house-to-house search was being made for them.

Within an hour from the arrival of the third refugee there was another knocking at the door. Every family in the city was now behind barred doors, so no suspicion was aroused upon finding this door closed and securely locked. This allowed time for each refugee to find some dark corner in the house, none venturing far from some exit for possible escape.

Ding Cu Geng stood behind the door as it was opened, a pistol in each hand, ready to fight his way to liberty if that became necessary. This man had been trapped time and again in equally hazardous positions, and had always cleared a way through the soldiers, who looked upon him as possessing a charmed life. He was now calmly ready for any eventuality.

When the door was opened the spokesman of the squad of soldiers said, "Mr. —, we are very sorry to trouble you, but we are reliably informed that the man we are looking for is in this house, and we have come with orders to arrest him."

My friend calmly answered, "If I have committed any offense I am ready to be arrested, but it would be interesting to know who sent you here to arrest me."

The soldier now spoke in a rather apologetic tone saying, "We are not come to arrest you, for we have never heard a word against you. It is bandit chief Ding Cu Geng we come to arrest. We have been told on reliable authority that he is in hiding in your house, but if you say that he is not here, of course, that settles it."

Without hesitancy enough to cause suspicion, the preacher replied, "I do not say that the chief is not in my house, and if you have reason to think that he is, step right in and make a thorough search." So saying, he moved aside, motioning the soldiers into the house, adding, "When it comes to the point where I have to go out and look up bandits for guests in my home I will not be so willing to have my house searched."

Instead of entering the open door the soldiers retreated a few steps, completely baffled at the frankness of the man. One man said to the leader of the squad, "Rest assured that there is no bandit in that house or that man would not be so willing to have us search. Come on elsewhere, for we have been misinformed as to the house the man entered."

Two hours later other soldiers came and battered with the butts of their rifles upon the door. At the same instant two soldiers appeared at the back door, to find the preacher's wife coolly preparing some vegetables for cooking.

Again the front door was opened and the soldiers peered inside, saying, "We are looking for Ding Cu Geng and others who we are told are in hiding in your home, but it must be false as everything seems normal in your home."

The only reply to this statement was an invitation to the soldiers to step in and have a cup of tea, to which the leader bowed low saying, "We have not time, as we must find the bandit chief before he has a chance to slip out under cover of darkness."

After dusk the man insisted that the men must leave the house. He volunteered to go with them to a place where they could scale the city wall, assuring them he would much rather be found with them on the street than to have them found in his home. It was a trying ordeal through which my friend passed, but in relating it he said to me that he could not think of telling a direct lie. The man showed something of his real Christian character under a test many would not want to face.

My family and guests, Mr. and Mrs. Andrews, had just seated themselves at the table for the evening meal when one of the missionaries rushed into the room holding the calling card of the *taotai* in his hand and saying, "The *taotai* has sent up his card asking some of us to come down and save him. He is to be killed by the northern soldiers. Will you go?" directing his question to both Andrews and to me.

Late in the afternoon we had seen from our home on the hill long files of soldiers marching along both banks of the river. We knew that these were the soldiers who were expected. Unfortunately, the Hunan soldiers had opened fire from their barracks on the hill beside the mission hospital when the troops were ferrying across the river.

By good luck, or on account of poor marksmanship, there were no casualties, although the northerners became very much incensed on account of the character of the reception extended them.

Accordingly, they stormed the guards at the several yamens upon entering the city, disarming them, and sending an ultimatum to the commander, giving him until daylight in the morning in which to turn in all his guns and ammunition. It was after these men had entered the yamen of the *taotai*, plundering it, and attempting to shoot the *taotai* himself, that the appeal was hurried up to us by the terrified official.

It is here necessary for me to relate briefly an experience which I had had a few weeks previously, as it afterward seemed to us all that this experience paved the way for the big job we found ourselves entangled in on this dark and dangerous night.

The district superintendent of one of my districts had been captured by northern soldiers and impressed into service as a tracker for one of the big river boats en route to Yuki City. Of course the minister could not play boatman to the satisfaction of the exacting soldiers, so he was mercilessly beaten, and finally strung by his thumbs to the limb of a banyan tree as a warning to others who might try to escape the soldiers. He suffered far more indignities at the hands of these heartless soldiers than I am chronicling here.

The case was one that could easily have been reported to the American Consul, where redress could have been demanded, but both the preacher and the missionaries wished to avoid litigation. I was asked to call upon the commander of the troops in Yuki City and settle the case in an amicable way.

This episode necessitated several interviews with the commander, who felt very keenly the wrong that had been done by his men, and who appreciated the attitude of the missionaries in a matter which could easily have been pushed, according to the provisions of the treaty, to a point which would have been most uncomfortable for him.

Responding to the appeal of the *taotai* for help, I hurried from the supper table to join my fellow missionary. Always ready for whatever is on, Mr. Andrews volunteered to accompany us, being assured we would likely have some excitement before we got back. We all went unarmed, of course, although it was more than possible that we might need to defend ourselves before we got through with our adventure.

Calling for Dr. Trimble, who was at the hospital looking after the wounded carried in from the streets, we encountered the commander of the Hunan troops, from whom we learned both of the disarming of the guards at several yamens, and of the ultimatum which had been sent over demanding a surrender of all his guns and ammunition.

In response to our query as to what he would do, the man coolly replied, "I am going to fight, sirs, for I have as many soldiers as the northern commander has. The battle will open at the break of dawn. I have twelve hundred Hunan men at Kienning upon whom I can rely, and who are acting as an army in reserve. Yes, I mean to chase the northerners out of the city."

We now realized that our task was a difficult one, for we had far more to do than merely to save the life of the *taotai*. We had to save the city, for its destruction was certain if hostilities broke out between the two armies now occupying barracks within its walls.

We hurried first to the yamen of the *taotai*. At the outer door we were greeted by guards who roughly held us up with well directed bayonets. Mr. Bankhardt, who alone of the four could talk fluently the mandarin dialect, said in a most polite way that we had called to see the *taotai*. The answer was insolent, and to the effect that the *taotai* was not in his office. To a request that we then be allowed to see the commander of the northern troops came a gruff reply that this was impossible. We were then ordered to move on.

Things looked very gloomy indeed. It was evident that there was no hope of getting inside the *taotai*'s yamen that night. We, of course, thought that the commander was inside the yamen, and that the *taotai* was his prisoner of war. If hostilities were actually opened at daylight, as we had been assured they most certainly would be, the prisoner would be disposed of during the night, and, judging by the message sent up to us less than an hour before, we all felt pretty certain that we knew what the disposition would be. If we were to do anything, we dared not delay long.

We were still standing in the presence of the insolent sentries discussing the situation in English, trying to devise some plan whereby we could see either the *taotai* or the northern commander, when a soldier came rushing by carrying an apology for a lantern. Fortunately for the whole situation the lantern gave light enough to permit the man to see four foreigners standing among the sentries. The man walked around our group holding the lantern close to the face of each of us. To my surprise, he paused in front of me, staring long into my face. I was in no humor to put up with such insolence, so was much relieved when the man smiled and spoke to me in perfect Foochow dialect saying: "This looks like Mr. Caldwell. Yes, to be sure, it is he."

I turned to the man, addressing him politely, and asked him where he had ever seen me, and how he knew me. To my question he replied, "When you called upon General Ciu in Yuki City to discuss the matter of the swinging tip by the thumbs of the Rev. Ngu I was present, serving as bodyguard; and when the general returned your call at the church I accompanied him, acting as interpreter for him and you. You remember me now, do you not?"

Yes, I did remember the man now, and recalled how I had wondered at the time how a northerner could speak such perfect Foochow language. We talked together for a few minutes with the soldier, from whom I learned that the commander in charge of the northern troops who had just entered the city was the same General Ciu whom I had interviewed several times in connection with the mal-treatment of the district superintendent. It was clear to all of us that there was decided hope for us in this fact, if it were but possible to effect an interview with the general.

I finally said in a low tone, so that the sentries could not possibly hear, "We have some exceedingly important matters to discuss with the commander. Our business is of a character that very greatly concerns the general. Can you possibly effect an interview without delay?"

Taking our calling cards the man hurried away, asking us to remain where we were until he returned. He dashed out into the open street and out of sight.

Our wait in the gloom with the sullen sentries was not as long as we had anticipated it might be, for there was soon to be heard the hurried clattering of heavy shoes on the cobblestone pavement of the street, from which there hurried up a uniformed figure with a glimmering light. It proved to be our soldier-messenger returning all dressed up in his regimentals. Approaching us he merely whispered, "Follow me, and I will take you to the general."

We followed the man out in the streets again and through the darkness from whence we had come. Our guide moved at a rapid pace while we stumbled along in the darkness in our endeavors to keep up. Stopping in front of a building we knew to be the Guild Hall the man shouted loudly, "The American teachers are here," whereupon we all filed into the building without further ceremony. Crossing the inner court we were met by the man we were so earnestly seeking.

We were then ushered by the general into a group seated around a table holding a council of war preparatory to the daylight attack upon the Hunan forces. The greetings extended each of us by General Ciu were cordial and of a reassuring nature, for it seemed to all of us that he appeared for some reason to be glad that we had come.

Formalities were brief, and tea drinking was dispensed with entirely, though before each of us was placed a cup of steaming brew. We immediately plunged into the matter for which we had sought the interview, making it plain that the peace of the city was heavy upon our hearts.

The response of the general to our solicitations for the safety of the city were so generous as to become embarrassing. As I was the only one of the four with whom he was acquainted, he called our guide forward to interpret. This was a relief to all of us, since his Mandarin was of a local type common to some locality in the north, and the change gave three of us an opportunity to understand perfectly all that was said.

We were kept busy framing up answers to his rapid fire questions, he supposing, of course, that we had come to represent the commander of the Hunan forces, and that we were in a position to answer questions concerning him.

"Where is the commander of the rebels?" asked the general.

"The bandits have been bravely dispersed by the Hunan commander, and their leader is not to be found in the

city," we replied. Continuing we suggested that as it was
not yet dark when the general entered the city he surely
must have seen the dead bandits where they fell. "Commander Ho of the Hunan forces," we told him, "has not
even found time to bury the rebel dead."

"Where is this brave Hunan commander that he has
not appeared to extend to me a welcome to this city?"
growled the northerner.

To this question we could only reply that doubtless
the commander was busy in some part of the city, adding,
"He has been relentlessly chasing down bandits almost
all day."

Here the general turned to us with the demand, "Who
fired upon my men as they were crossing the river?"

We were not wholly unprepared for this question, however, for we felt sure that sooner or later it would be asked.

"Commander Ho's men fired upon you," was our reply,
and before the general could get in a word we waxed elo-
quent on this point, saying that from our homes on the
hill we could see the two lines of khaki clad men moving
along the river like ants for multitude. How easy a thing it
would have been for even us, we suggested, with our field
glasses, to mistake these moving columns for bandits bent
upon revenge for the heavy losses of their fellows in the city.

"If we with field glasses could not be certain of your
identity, how much more difficult would it be for Commander Ho to be certain, since the uniforms of the bandits
were the same color as those of your men!"

Finally we declared, "That Commander Ho did fire upon
you even after you were well under the shadow of the
wails of the city only proves what we say about his deter-
mination to protect the city from the bandits at all cost."

So, one after another, we fired our broadsides of this
kind, at all times keeping safely within the bounds of the
truth, until we saw plainly a change in the whole attitude
of the general.

Just at this juncture the most psychological thing happened. Commander Ho himself suddenly appeared upon the scene. Entering unattended, he advanced and greeted the general graciously. He must have known that we were at that particular time in the place, for otherwise it would have been a desperately daring thing to do. Even as it was we did not know what the outcome would be.

The young commander advanced to the center of the room with perfect military bearing and courtesied low to all present, in response to which we all arose and bowed low. Everything was tense, of course, as this man advanced a few paces and saluted General Ciu.

As if by common agreement, we four foreigners arose and closed in around the two. One of our number advanced to the side of Commander Ho, and, placing a hand upon his shoulder, said, "How very timely is your coming," and, turning to General Ciu added, "This is he of whom we have been talking, the brave defender of this city. To this man is due the credit for the peace and quiet this city enjoys to-night. Even the dead bandits upon the streets testify to this."

We were now all requested by the general to resume our seats at the council table, and quite informally General Ciu requested the newcomer to take a seat close to him. Before the lapse of another hour all danger of a conflict between the troops of the two commanders was dispelled, and we four Americans breathed easy for the first time during the evening.

Soon we found the two military men asking our advice as to the best way in which to handle the situation in the city. Our work thus far had been signally successful, and all possible danger of the battle which had been staged for the morrow had been definitely removed.

The weasel-eyed mayor was present and had been spending a good part of the past two hours trying to find out from one of us where the *taotai* was in hiding. All he could get out of any of us was, "Yes, we have an idea where he is and probably could persuade him to come out when the time comes."

This only aggravated the anxious mayor, who was the more insistent upon one or the other of us accompanying him to the *taotai*'s place of hiding and inviting him to the council in the guild hall. We had learned from the general enough to know that the *taotai* had not been killed, nor was he at that time a prisoner. That was enough for the present, so we just let that question rest. Finally we ignored the mayor entirely, refusing to discuss matters with him at all. We even intimated what we suspected was the real motive in his seeming overanxious attitude about the whereabouts of the *taotai*. This quieted the traitorous rascal for the rest of the evening.

Naturally, everyone suspected that the *taotai* was in hiding in some of our mission buildings, and we were quite content to have it that way, since in this fact alone lay his safety during the night.

It was now midnight, the two military commanders were busily engaged discussing plans for the morrow, so we made ready to return to our homes. The general came forward and thanked us for the interest we had manifested in the serious situation, requesting us to return at nine o'clock in the forenoon on the next day to advise with him concerning certain other important matters.

We all knew full well what was in the mind of the general, for he too thought the *taotai* was enjoying the hospitality of one of our homes. He had been filled up with reports concerning the man by the mayor, who confidently expected to prove his own allegiance to the north, and consequently be appointed *taotai* in place of the deposed man.

Our interview with the general and his men the following morning was none the less interesting, nor was the work that we accomplished any less important. Everything centered around the *taotai*.

The general was childish in his grievance because the *taotai* did not come out and "receive him" in proper fashion. We pointed out that one of the soldiers the evening before had pointed a rifle at the breast of the man and fired in an attempt to kill the *taotai*, his life only being saved by one of the disarmed soldiers of Commander Ho knocking the gun barrel high in the air.

To all our argument the general paid but little heed, even going so far as to justify the conduct of his men. Thus we see-sawed for more than an hour, the general insisting upon our disclosing the whereabouts of the *taotai*, and we in turn insisting upon an absolute guarantee that the man would not be misused.

Finally, the general said, with what might be termed military emphasis, "The *taotai* must meet me right here in his yamen. I am a guest in this city and he must respect me as such. I will only talk with him after he has received me according to the etiquette which should be used in receiving one of my high station."

We only insisted upon a guarantee of safe conduct and that the man should not be maltreated, else we would not be a party to advising him to come out of his place of refuge. Again, the inference among the military men was that the man was in hiding in one of our homes. The thing now began to have an amusing aspect, for these men were so completely fooled into thinking something which none of us had so much as intimated.

We were getting nowhere in our deliberations, so something must be done. I knew a timely card to play, for I knew the reports over Yuki way about how this man found difficulty controlling his soldiers. A number of small squads, in fact, had recently deserted and turned bandit, and I knew it, and he knew that I knew it. And, too, it will be remembered, his soldiers had strung up one of my district superintendents. This alone reflected very unfavorably upon the man.

I arose and said with considerable feeling, "General, what I have heard about you and your soldiers is undoubtedly true. I did not believe it when I heard it in Yuki, but evidently it is very true."

We all made a move as if to leave his presence.

"What have you heard?" bawled the officer. "What is it you are beginning to believe?"

I then told him that I had heard it said that he could not control his men, suggesting that this thing must be true since he dare not guarantee even safe conduct for the *taotai* whom he urged us to call from his hiding place.

In answer to all that was said the general shouted a summons to an attendant and gave some rapid orders in a language I could not understand. Within a few minutes a lieutenant stood before him who was directed to call a corporal to take a squad of men to escort the *taotai* through the streets. There was now no question about safe conduct for the man we all very highly respected.

When the escort arrived we suggested that, since the general had given his word in this way, we felt the escort was not necessary, for the general's word is all the guarantee anyone should ask. This pleased the man, who began to give orders for the return of the escort to their places.

According to custom in China in cases of disorder of a character such as this, where all business is suspended and shops closed, the mayor should pass along the streets shouting to the people to open their doors and resume business. This serves as a guarantee to the people, but to do this in this particular instance would be humiliating to the mayor, for all the merchants knew full well the part that he had played in the whole affair which came so near costing the city dearly.

We suggested that the escort which was offered to bring the *taotai* should accompany the mayor, who should go out and make the announcement to the merchants along the street, bidding them to resume business. To this suggestion the general readily agreed, while the mayor scowled. Within less than ten minutes the mayor was well along the main business street on his mission, while one of the group who had withdrawn unnoticed ushered the *taotai* into the presence of the general.

We remained for another hour, and until every possible breach between the general and *taotai* was definitely averted. We then accompanied the two up the street to the guild hall, where a general council with all the leading gentry of the city was held. At this juncture we withdrew, feeling that our work of the past twelve hours or so had been really very much worth while.

In due time we received an official communication from the Chamber of Commerce thanking us for the timely service we had rendered at a time when the whole city seemed very much endangered.

The *taotai* remains a very much loved local governor in our city. He said to a bishop of the Methodist Church in 1921: "I was assigned to this station by the government in order that I might preserve peace and order, protecting both the property and lives of everyone. Instead of my protecting the lives of the people, including the few foreigners living in this city, they in turn not only saved my life, but they saved the city as well."

This is just one instance where the missionary rendered a service to the people and country which was a bit outside the recognized program of missionary activity. The mistake which is being made is that so many people can only think of the missionary in connection with some program for stereotyped preaching of the gospel, forgetting that preaching, administering to the sick, or directing a program for the education of the people are but three of the many ways he serves the cause of the church and humanity.

The modern missionary, to be most successful, must be one who can do a lot more than that particular kind of work for which he has signed up with one of the mission boards. True, this is a day of highly specialized work in any country, and possibly this thing is just as much so on the foreign field as in the homelands, but at the same time the missionary cannot get away from a far greater service to humanity than can be measured in terms of years preparing for some special form of work.

I recall only a few months before I left China in 1922, when visiting a locality where there were continual conflicts between bandits and soldiers, being asked to perform a duty of a rather new kind even to me, who had been trying to render almost every kind of service to the people during this period of more than twenty years.

There had been a battle ten miles from the city in which the soldiers were badly beaten, leaving a number of their dead, among whom was a specially commissioned deputy from the Tuchün in Foochow. The defeat itself was humiliating enough for the commander of the northern troops, but not to be able to bury the dead was that which gave the general greatest concern, for it reflected very great discredit upon him. The men were lying where they fell, and had been there for ten days at the time that I visited Yuki City. The stench was so great as to close the roads to traffic.

The bandits had established a camp within watching distance from the dead soldiers and were defying the commander in his endeavor to secure the bodies. Several contingents of soldiers had been sent out for the purpose of bringing the dead into the city. One such attempt only added three more to the number of the abandoned dead.

The commander called me, imploring me to use my good offices to move the bandit to give up the dead soldiers. He said, "It is humiliating enough to me to have been so decisively defeated, and to have to report these men and officers dead, but if I cannot return the bodies to their own people, if so requested, I will lose face and possibly my commission."

I knew that I could not get these bodies immediately removed into the city, but believed that I could get them put into coffins and properly cared for. This I undertook to do, and did do, very much to the satisfaction of the distressed commander of the troops, but more to the comfort of the people living adjacent to the terrible sight.

Such, possibly, would be one of the last types of service expected of a missionary, but it is in just such seemingly little things that often a worth-while service can be rendered. Where such service is freely given it is no difficult thing to find a hearing when the gospel message is offered to the people. All such services can be used as points of contact for rendering that greatest of all service, which is bringing men and women into saving touch with Jesus Christ.

Appendix

The Trail of the Blue Tiger

Roy Chapman Andrews

In South China, the weird legends of men and animals come from the people of the hills. They find their way to the coast where their telling often lures men into the jungle of the back country.

I had followed just such a legend to Futsing, the story of a blue tiger. To me it was still not a completely credible legend, though it had been substantiated by friends in both America and China. But still, I told myself as I lay on my cot that night, I would never really believe a blue tiger existed until I saw one myself.

My thoughts were suddenly interrupted. A shriek pierced the night. There was a snarl, then the agonized, stifled cry of a child. I leaped to my feet. "—, Harry, what is it?" Harry Caldwell was already up, jamming cartridges into his rifle. "Tiger, I think; Hurry."

We ran across the orchard to a house a hundred yards away. The courtyard swarmed with screaming Chinese. A woman sat cross-legged on the floor rocking back and forth, tearing handfuls of hair out by the roots. "*Ai-ya, ai-ya,*" she wailed. "My baby. The black tiger. It took my baby. Kill it, *Shen-shung*. Kill the black tiger."

Harry talked rapidly with the terrified natives. "Get lanterns," he shouted. "Come with me."

Edited from: *True: The Man's Magazine*, January 1950.

We dashed out the gate and across the rice dikes, followed by a dozen men. Breathlessly, Harry told me what had happened.

"Family eating—baby playing in the court—suddenly the tiger leaped through the door and grabbed the child. It stood for a moment and then leaped over the wall. There's one chance in a thousand it may drop the baby when it sees the lights—but he would be dead—tiger'll head for the big ravine. Natives called it black, but I'm sure it's the blue devil—that's where it lives. This makes sixteen for it, sixteen people in two years!"

We rushed on in the darkness. For a mile we followed a narrow path beside the rice fields. Where the sword grass shut in like a wall on either side, a bloody rag hung on a thorn bush; a few feet beyond lay a tiny baby's shoe.

Caldwell stopped. "No use going farther. The poor little fellow's done for. We'll have to wait until tomorrow."

We turned back to the village, but not to sleep. The wailing of the family kept the night alive with the sounds of death. Moreover, our tent was pitched in the orchard and there might be another tiger on the prowl. I couldn't have slept anyway, so I smoked my pipe until early morning, while Harry sat in the tent door, relaxed, but alert and watchful with a Hi-Power Savage rifle across his knees. There was plenty of time to talk and think.

I studied Caldwell curiously, for we had just met, after months of correspondence. Six feet tall, spare and hard as a trained athlete, with a flashing smile that seldom left his face in repose, intensely alive, bursting with enthusiasm. That was the man with whom I had come to hunt the blue tiger. A missionary, too, though he didn't resemble any I had ever seen.

It was Captain Thomas Holcomb of the U. S. Marine Corps, now U. S. minister to South Africa, who first spoke of him to me at the American Museum of Natural History in New York.

"He is an amazing man," Tom said. "An effective missionary, a good amateur naturalist and the finest field rifle shot

I've ever seen. I hunted with him. He kills tigers with a .303 Savage rifle. Better get in touch with him if you're going to China."

This was in 1916. I was planning an expedition to the mountains of the Tibetan frontier and Yunnan for the American Museum of Natural History, so I wrote Caldwell at Futsing, China. His reply was vibrant with the personality of the man and told an amazing story.

There was a strange tiger there; not yellow like the ordinary tiger but Maltese blue. Perhaps it was a new species. Why didn't I stop and try to get it on my way to Yunnan?

Letter after letter followed, always full of accounts of the blue tiger. In spite of what Caldwell said, I didn't believe it was a new species, but rather a melanistic phase of the yellow tiger. Melanism, the opposite of albinism, is an excess of coloring matter in the skin and occurs in many animals. But a blue or black tiger was unknown to the zoological world. Caldwell's word could not be doubted, and the museum authorities agreed that the story certainly should be investigated.

I knew I would have to stop at Futsing. Enthusiastically I talked about it with Dr. William T. Hornaday, then director of the New York Zoological Park, in the Bronx. "Perhaps," I told him, "I can bring it back alive. When it dies, the museum will get the skin and skeleton anyway. Would you be interested?"

Hornaday smiled. "Would I be interested to have the only blue tiger in the world? Don't ask silly questions! I'll get you a trap if you'll try to use it." He did. He had a trap especially made for me. It looked as though it would hold an elephant.

With trap and gear, I set off for China, after Tom Holcomb's final words about Harry Caldwell had put my mind at ease. I needn't worry, Tom had assured me when I expressed misgivings at spending weeks in the field with a missionary. Caldwell was a "he man" if there ever was one. He had spent his boyhood in the Tennessee mountains near Chattanooga. "If he wasn't born with a squirrel rifle in his hands," Tom said, "he got hold of one soon after. He's another Sergeant

York so far as shooting is concerned, and he's certainly done a wonderful job as a missionary."

On my way down the China coast I heard much more of Caldwell; everyone seemed to know of him. His exploits were legends among "old hands" in China. A bishop told me how Caldwell had opened to Christian teaching a community of a hundred settlements—more than half a million violently anti-foreign Chinese—by killing a man-eating tiger that had been ravaging their villages.

That was the opening wedge. Before long, other villages had asked his help, and his fame had spread. But it was not only for the killing of tigers. Because of his reputation for courage, honesty and fair dealing, he sometimes had acted as middleman in settling disputes, and once had saved a village from terrible slaughter by going alone to a bandit camp and persuading the chief to take his men back to the hills. The chief had been misinformed, he told them; the money they had demanded to ransom the village was not there, and he offered himself as hostage until his words were proved.

I thought of these things as I sat in the tent looking at Caldwell. Harry turned around.

"It was in that ravine," he said, "that I killed my first tiger. I used buckshot, but believe me, I'll never try that again. She was a big tigress and had eaten a boy the day before. The elders asked me to rid them of her, but the bearer with my load and rifle hadn't arrived and, like a fool, I went out with only my shotgun. I'd never seen a tiger in the wild, and had no idea how hard they are to kill. It seemed to me that buckshot at close range would be all right.

"I staked a goat on an abandoned terrace and sat down behind some bushes off to one side. The tigress came out almost immediately on a grass-covered dike about a hundred yards away, but she seemed to suspect danger. For more than an hour she crouched there just like a great tabby cat, sometimes pushing one loot forward as though about to move, but each time drawing it back again. She looked awfully big and I wished I hadn't come, but I couldn't get out except by passing right below her. There was a confounded brain-fever bird on a tree above me, and it kept giving that rising, breathless call that drives people crazy. It got on my nerves so I could hardly keep from screaming.

"Finally, the tigress got up and circled to reach a small path—they'll never attack through unbroken tangle if they can get to a trail. She had to cross a small bare space—it was only about twenty yards—but apparently she didn't like being in the open. She flattened just like a snake, her chin and throat touching the ground, and slithered along with no body motion except for a quivering of her shoulders and hips. Yet she went awfully fast. As soon as she was in cover again, she made three flying leaps up the narrow terraces toward the goat. The last one brought her face to face with me about twelve feet away. She stood there, snarling. Her yellow and black head looked big as a haystack, and her eyes simply blazed. I let her have both barrels in the face and neck.

"I thought the buckshot would be in an almost solid mass at that range, and would knock her cold, but she only slipped backward off the terrace and didn't fall. Blood streamed over her head, and she shook it out of her eyes and then slowly walked off into a patch of sword grass. I was scared, for I didn't have any more buckshot cartridges—only No. 4 shot. So I sat tight for half an hour, and then worked up the hill through the bush and back to the village.

"The bearer was there with my rifle when I arrived, but it was almost dark and I didn't dare go out that evening. Next day I followed the blood trail with the natives and found her dead nearly half a mile away. Her whole face and neck were full of buckshot, most of which were flattened against the heavy bones. I think she bled to death.

"When the Chinese brought her back to the village, the mother of the boy she had eaten began beating her with a stick, screaming curses. I kept only the skin for myself, and gave the body to the village elders. Every drop of blood was sopped up with rags which they tied about their necks to ward off disease and personal devils. The meat was sold as medicine. Anyone who ate a small piece was supposed to acquire some of the tiger's courage. The bones, whiskers and claws they stewed up into a kind of jelly; after it cooled and hardened, it was molded into pills and sold to Chinese druggists in Futsing at a high price. That tigress brought the village nearly four hundred dollars. But shotguns are out for me, I don't mind telling you. That one experience was enough."

"I should think it would be, but," I laughed, "I believe the .22 Hi-Power you've got is just about as bad. It's plain —ed foolishness to use that little bullet, if you don't mind my saying so. It hasn't enough weight or shocking power for dangerous game."

Caldwell smiled. "That's what a lot of people say. I killed eight or ten tigers with the .303, and, thought it was grand, but the first time I ever fired this rifle I killed a tiger. You ought to have seen what that tiny bullet did to him. He was a big tiger, too—a man-eater that had killed several people in this very village. I staked a goat, as usual, but instead of coming out where I thought he would, the tiger appeared on a barren ridge more than a hundred yards away. It was already half dark, and I couldn't see plainly through the sights, so I walked into the open and moved up. The tiger saw me instantly, of course, and stood there switching his tail with ears laid flat against his head. I expected him to charge at any moment, but I had to keep on going until I was close enough to shoot in the bad light. If I had turned back then, he'd have come for me. Finally I was only thirty yards away. It was too dark to pick any vital spot, so I just fired at the body. The beast lunged into the air, twisted and came down dead as a herring. The bullet had caught him behind the ribs and went through the stomach. His intestines were messed up as though they'd been put through a sausage grinder. He had just eaten a dog and the stomach was full of meat."

"Well," I told him, "next time you use a .22 you probably won't be here to tell about it, unless you hit it in the head or neck. You don't realize that you were extraordinarily lucky. You say your bullet went through the stomach which was full of dog. To my mind what happened was this: the high-velocity bullet striking that extended stomach set up a terrific gas explosion which ruptured the intestines. That was what killed your tiger. I've shot woodchucks with a hard-nose .22 Hi-Power bullet, and they just blow up if I get them through the body when the stomach is packed with food, if it's empty, I lose my 'chuck."

Caldwell remained unconvinced. "Maybe you're right. But," he grinned, "next time I won't shoot him in the stomach. I'll hit him in the head."

Later I learned that Caldwell did kill other tigers with the .22 Hi-Power, but I don't know how many. Even though he once took on five of them with the .303 Savage and only six cartridges, and killed two, he gave up the .303 and used the .22 Hi-Power exclusively. After I had hunted with him for months in China and Mongolia and saw him kill flying birds with a rifle, I realized he could just about pick—on any animal's body—the hair he wanted to split.

But the night's experience had made me eager to hear more about the murderous blue tiger and I prodded Harry.

"I've seen it twice," he said. "The first time it wasn't twenty yards from me, but I had only a shotgun. I came on it suddenly, lying right in the path in the sun like a great Maltese cat. While I was watching, it got up slowly and stood for a moment in the trail, then turned around three times. I thought it was going to lie down again, but it stretched, humped its back, and jumped into the bushes. I had a perfect view; could have hit it with a stone. It's really beautiful. The ground color of its body is Maltese, changing into light blue on the lower sides and belly. The stripes are black and well defined like those on a yellow tiger.

"The second time was last year, and I had it absolutely cold in the sights of my rifle, but I didn't dare shoot. I had staked a goat in an open space near the lair, and saw the blue tiger creeping up, but from the other side of the ravine. I was just going to fire when I realized it was stalking two boys asleep under an old dike right below it. If I had wounded the beast, it would have certainly rolled down on the boys. I couldn't chance it, so I stood up and yelled. It turned about facing me, snarled and then walked slowly into the grass."

That was the animal we were going to track; the daring, cunning and lucky blue, which had twice eluded Caldwell. But we weren't to set out until mid-afternoon. The baby was so small, Harry explained, that it wasn't a big meal for the tiger, and by evening it would be looking for something else, we hoped.

So when the sun rose in a hot red ball over the hills, and the village stirred to life, Caldwell and I pulled the tent flaps and slept. At noon we were up, and before 3 o'clock were on our way through the rice fields, dragging two reluctant goats, a mother and her kid. At the entrance to a narrow ravine, Caldwell halted.

"This is where the blue tiger lives and I'll bet it's home. We'll tie the goats in this little open space and get behind those bushes."

"But," I protested, "it'll be right in our laps when it comes out!"

"Can't be helped. There isn't any other spot. I know this lair like the palm of my hand. There's where I killed my first tiger with the shotgun, right on that terrace."

It was a devilish place, a deep cut in the mountain choked with thorny vines and sword grass. Three or four dark tunnels twisted snakelike back into the murderous growth. "Tiger paths," Caldwell said, laconically. "I crawled up that one on the right for about twenty feet one day. Found a sort of room with bones of all kinds and heaps of pangolin scales. Tigers love pangolins. Branch tunnels went off in three directions. Then, I realized what a foolish thing I'd done. My hair began to prickle and I backed out in a hurry."

We crouched behind a clump of bushes, half buried in sword grass. Fifteen feet away, the goats blatted incessantly;

otherwise there wasn't a sound in the lair. A sweet stench of rotting flesh drifted out of the tunnel's mouth. It nauseated me; Harry wrinkled his nose in disgust. For three hours we sat. I watched the shadows steal slowly down the ravine and reach a lone palm tree on the opposite side. My watch said half past 6; that meant another hour of waiting, not more, for night comes swiftly in those South China hills.

Just as I was about to shift my cramped body, I heard the faint crunching sound of a stone rolled under a heavy weight. The mother goat bleated in terror, tugging frantically at her rope. Harry's shoulder touched mine. "It's coming," he breathed.

I was half kneeling, my heavy rifle pushed forward. A drop of sweat trickled down my nose, divided, and ran into the corners of my mouth. I could taste the salt of the sweat. Another drop started above my left eye and I blinked, frantically. Caldwell sat like a stone Buddha, the stock of his tiny rifle nestled against his cheek. Ten minutes dragged by; it seemed ten hours.

"—," I thought, "why doesn't it come?"

Suddenly all hell broke loose on the opposite hill. Shouts and yells, beating of pans, stones rolling down the slope. A small army of woodcutters swarmed over the crest on to the trail. The noise was to frighten tigers. They did a good job for, with a rumbling growl, the blue tiger turned back into the depths of his lair. There it was. I had only one fleeting glimpse, but I saw it was really blue. I got to my feet and stood silently for a long moment just looking at the Chinese. Then I let loose. At the end of my spectacular oration, Harry rolled his eyes and pronounced a fervent "amen."

We were disappointed, but Caldwell explained that the blue tiger would turn up again. "It operates in about three or four villages, here and on the other side of the mountain, but seldom stays more than a day or two in any one place."

We had to wait only a day when a breathless Chinese arrived from a village four miles away.

"The black tiger came right into the street," he shouted at us, "and grabbed a dog. It threw him over its shoulder like a sack of rice and ran off to the hills. Everyone followed, yelling and beating pans and just inside the grass, on an old dike, it dropped the dog. He's there; we found him."

Caldwell was electrified. "This time we'll get it alive, Roy. If a tiger hasn't finished its kill, it will always come back after dark."

We hurried to the village. Dozens of excited men wanted to show us the dog, but Caldwell selected only two and told the others to make a cage of heavy bamboo trunks.

"We'll catch the black tiger for you tonight," he said. "I speak the truth." They looked dubious, but examined my trap with enormous interest. I clamped the vises on the springs, screwed them down and set it.

We found the dog lying beside a tree on a terrace about five feet wide, just above the open rice fields. His skull was crushed, probably from the first blow of the tiger's paw, but only teeth marks showed on the body. "It couldn't be better," Harry said. We buried the trap on the terrace and fastened the dog to the tree with heavy wire.

We slept that night in the village. After sunrise, at least fifty men, women and boys accompanied us to the trap, bearing a cage strong enough to hold a gorilla. Harry and I halted the crowd a hundred yards away, and approached the terrace, rifles ready. Silence.

"What's wrong, Roy? He ought to be raising Cain."

Foot by foot we crept forward, but not a sound broke the stillness of the jungle. At last we could see the trap. No tiger—and the dog was gone! We stared in dumb amazement.

"It just can't be," Harry said. But it was, all too plainly. The blue tiger had approached from above, as we expected, dropped its fore feet on the terrace, reached over and lifted our securely wired dog from the tree as though he had been tied with string. Then it had eaten him comfortably on the upper dike a few feet away. The claw marks were within an inch of the trap pan. Just one inch more and we'd have had it!

The villagers crowded about like a jury to examine the evidence. Collectively they shook their heads and old Wang, elder of the village, delivered the verdict.

"Some years ago, *Sheng*, our villager, as you well know, killed his father. He was given the 'Death of a Thousand Cuts,' but nothing was done by our people to atone for his crime. The gods were offended. Now they have sent this black beast to harass our dwelling place. It is not a common tiger. No one can trap or kill an Evil Spirit."

Harry and I walked back to camp saying little. We had lost face with the villagers. Harry thought of its effect on his missionary work; I was thinking of what a sensation the blue tiger would have caused in New York. To make it worse, a runner waited at the village with a cable from Dr. Hornaday. "How about the blue tiger?" it read. "When may we expect him?"

Three days later, the tiger killed again seven miles from our camp. It had been asleep on a grass-covered terrace when a dozen fuel gatherers disturbed it. The enraged beast leaped to its feet and dashed into the group, striking right and left with its great paws. One man's skull was crushed; another's head ripped half off his shoulders; a third landed ten feet away on a lower dike with a broken neck. Then the tiger leaped to an abandoned terrace, stood for a moment, turned and slunk off into the grass. It made no attempt to drag off any of its victims: apparently the killing was out of sheer bad temper at being disturbed.

When word reached us at 3 o'clock, Caldwell and I almost ran the seven miles. "It's sure to return this afternoon," Harry said. "We've got to get there before it comes."

For two wretched hours we sat in the broiling sun, crouched behind a bush near the terrace where the man had been killed. —, it was hot! The thermometer had registered plus 106 degrees in the shade when we left, and the humidity must have been 80 per cent. I didn't feel at all well. Jagged black patches darted before my eyes and violent nausea doubled me up in uncontrollable spasms of retching and coughing. Every time I went into my act, the sounds whacked back like rifle shots in the stillness of the jungle. Of course, that ruined our chance again. Just as night was closing in, the vague outline of the blue tiger showed against a background of feathery bamboo on the opposite slope, but before either of us could shoot, it faded from sight like a black ghost. "The Great Invisible," I remarked, sadly. "That's what he ought to be called."

My heatstroke was a bad one, and for a week I lay in camp under a tree, racked with fever, headache and nausea. Finally, I had to leave for Hong Kong to outfit for a year's expedition along the Tibetan frontier, but ten days of Caldwell's vacation still remained. He stayed on for another go at the Great Invisible and it very nearly cost him his life. I've set down the story as he told it to me later.

"A few days after you left," he said, "the blue tiger did something I wouldn't have believed possible. It jumped into a cowpen beside a house, killed a yearling heifer and leaped out with the dead animal in its mouth. The farmer and his wife saw the whole performance. I measured the fence; it was twelve feet high. My Chinese hunter, Da Da, and I found the remains of the heifer only half eaten about two miles away. The carcass was in a bad place, a very bad place. Four or five trails led to a little open space in thick jungle where the heifer lay, and the only way we could see it was by sitting in one of the paths. We didn't dare touch it.

"I said to Da Da, 'I don't like this at all. You know a tiger always moves along a trail if he can. It might come down this one.'

"Da Da looked about, 'But, *Sheng-shung*, with all the wide world, and all these other paths, why should it come this way?'

"I still didn't like it, but there was no other spot. We'd been watching about an hour, and the sun was bright, when I thought I heard the low rumble of thunder. Da Da heard it, too, and we both looked at the sky; there wasn't a cloud. Then the rumble came again and this time it ended in a snarl. The blue tiger was right behind us in the grass! I knew it was close enough to spring, too, else it wouldn't have growled. We couldn't see the beast, but I was sure any sudden move would bring it on us. There was just one thing to do; take it by surprise. All tigers are afraid of the human voice—it is about the only thing they are afraid of. I twisted around very, very slowly and the tiger snarled again. I suppose it didn't spring because it was completely taken aback to find us there. Suddenly, I yelled and leaped straight at it, but caught my foot in a vine and sprawled on my face, arms outstretched. This, you'll hardly believe, Roy, but it's true: *my left hand actually slapped the tiger on its nose!* The beast went right over backward, whirled, and in one jump disappeared in the grass.

"I never was so scared in my life: I couldn't have fired even if I hadn't dropped the rifle. Da Da and I stood there shaking for a time, and then both of us got awfully sick. We could hardly walk back to the village."

That was the last time either Caldwell or I hunted the blue tiger. After his vacation, he went up the Min River to a mission station at Yenping, and although he returned to Futsing from time to time and killed other tigers, he never saw the blue devil again. But the Great Invisible, or another blue like it, still exists. Caldwell, recently returned to this country, brought with him reports from the natives that a giant blue tiger is again terrorizing villagers in the South China hills.

Publisher's Note

Today, the South China Tiger (*Panthera tigris amoyensis*) is critically endangered, with perhaps 30 left in the wild and less than 70 in captivity. Chinese conservationists are working to stave off its extinction. One organization, SaveChinasTigers.org, is attempting to breed and reintroduce these tigers back into their native homeland.

COACHWHIP PUBLICATIONS
COACHWHIPBOOKS.COM

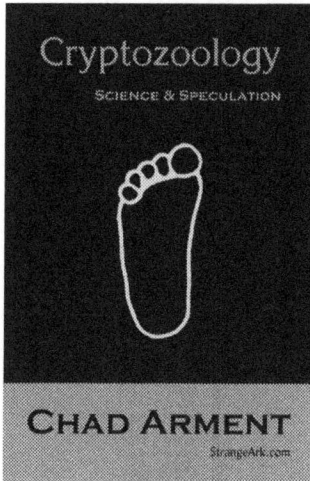

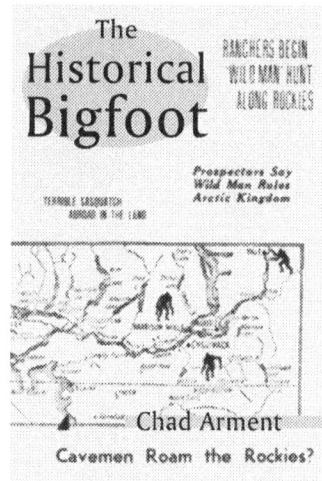

Cryptozoology: Science & Speculation (1-930585-15-2)

The Historical Bigfoot (1-930585-30-6)

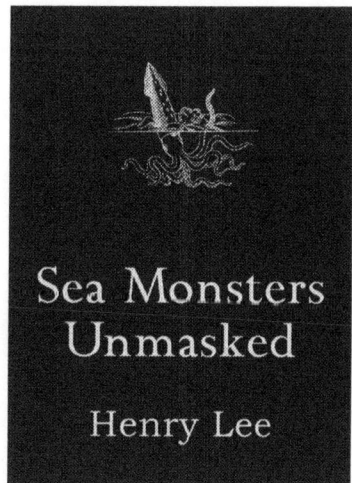

The Great Sea-Serpent (1-930585-36-5)

Sea Monsters Unmasked (1-930585-37-3)